Transplanting One Heart and
Transforming Many Others

DISPATCHES

FROM THE

HEART

ED AND PAIGE INNERARITY

RIVER GROVE
BOOKS

The names and identifying characteristics of persons referenced in this book have been changed to protect their privacy.

Published by River Grove Books
Austin, TX
www.rivergrovebooks.com

Distributed by River Grove Books

Design and composition by Greenleaf Book Group
Cover design by Greenleaf Book Group
Cover image © Hein Nouwens. Used under license from Shutterstock.com

Publisher's Cataloging-in-Publication data is available.

Print ISBN: 978-1-63299-179-9

eBook ISBN: 978-1-63299-180-5

First Edition

FOREWORD

This should be pretty straightforward, I thought. About twenty years into my career as a cardiologist, my friend Jim Kemper asked me to see his brother-in-law who had a problem that I have helped patients manage many, many times without significant issues. Modern medicine has made great strides in the last few years, and the treatment of congestive heart failure certainly has not lagged. I had not sent a patient for a transplant in my career.

Unfortunately, my friend Ed Innerarity broke that streak, followed by another of my longstanding patients shortly thereafter (if any of my patients are reading this, there have been no others; the wheels aren't falling off). The idea that he might be transplanted was a fairly distant concern. Sure, when I met him, he had some fairly concerning features with his family history and with his low resting heart function, but I'd seen this before.

The first six or so years that he was my patient, we mostly did what friends do—we fished, we visited, our families became very close friends. We argued about whether he should climb Half Dome in Yosemite with an ejection fraction of 20 percent and a defibrillator, but I lost (as did his wife, Paige, I think).

Sometimes, though, when you lose, you win. Rather than call me after he climbed Half Dome, he sent me a picture of him standing on a tongue of granite jutting out into space at the top, with the valley far, far below. That picture is on my desk at home. When I look at it, I am reminded of his indefatigable spirit. You are fortunate to see things like that in life. It helps you know what life can be.

After a long period of stability, Ed's status changed, and it became obvious that he would need to be considered for more aggressive treatment, including consideration for heart transplantation. But the more things changed, the more they seemed to stay the same. Ed and Paige have a remarkable relationship, and their courage and fortitude while they waited in Austin was conspicuously normal.

The day of his transplant, the three of us sat around and talked for a few hours, and most of what we talked about was what we usually talked about—our families, fishing, the day-to-day issues about what was going on with his care. Then Ed asked me, "So, David, what happens if the new heart doesn't start?"

The question surprised me. I know how to resuscitate people, just not in that particular circumstance. Rather than warble on about something I don't have specific expertise in, I quickly answered, "I don't know, Ed; they always start," and we moved on. Adding ambiguity to the transplant process at that moment, particularly by discussing the finer points of perioperative cardiac support, wasn't part of the therapeutic milieu that I envisioned, particularly with a heart on the way. And it didn't hurt that I had absolute faith in the people doing the operation and the care he was to receive.

Well, the new heart started. And the story goes on. Ed is eternally grateful to his donor and the family of the donor. All of his family and friends are too. He is the best advertisement for a donor card there could be. He has touched so many people in so many ways and continues to do so. Life with him is an adventure, in no small part because he is like a hybrid of Leonardo da Vinci and Huck Finn, a rare blend of aptitude and moxie. A unique life, with multiple iterations.

But the best part of the story is the story itself. Ed and Paige's journey together, their courage and love for each other, the community that we all shared and continue to share. It was, and is, a remarkable experience for so many of us. Someone should write a book about it.

David Terreson
Austin, Texas

PREFACE

"To live will be an awfully big adventure."

—PETER PAN

Ed, July 2, 2016

I am one of the lucky ones; I received a heart transplant. That was in the summer of 2015. After ninety-three days of waiting, a matching heart was found, and only hours later, the heart from a donor I currently know nothing about was beating strong in my chest. Almost immediately, my body responded positively. I was breathing on my own within thirty-six hours, my color improved dramatically, and I recall that I could hear a pounding in my ears when I woke from the surgery. It was the strong pulse created by my new heart.

I sent the emails in this book to my family and friends during my wait for my new heart and for the first year afterward. I consider it a journal of sorts, an outlet of major proportions, for sure—equal parts coping humor, medical observations, and reflections of a life nearly lost and then restored.

Nearly 3,500 heart transplants take place each year, about two-thirds of those in the United States, so there is nothing new, special, or unique about mine. In fact, it was my observation that the other men and women in my "transplant class" struggled more than I did. From my perspective, their stories were often more compelling than mine. Many of the others in my transplant class received an LVAD (left heart ventricular assist device, or heart mate) because they could not wait for a donated heart or they did not qualify. The LVAD might be a temporary bridge to a heart transplant or might be a "destination," meaning it was with them to the end. Others may have had heart attacks, multiple bypasses, or the failure of other organs at the same time they were in heart failure. Some days the clinic was littered with wheelchairs, oxygen bottles, and desperate patients. Many could not even walk across the room. The best hope for those with LVADs as a bridge was that after a minimum of six months off the transplant list, they might get a matching heart and have major surgery again. Others were often on a second heart mate with a host of related problems.

The difference, if any, was that I saw firsthand how my family and friends supported me, hurt for me, and did everything humanly possible to intervene for me. And possibly for the first time in my life, I watched as others helped me. The heart transplant, and all that led up to it, was the biggest challenge of my life, and it was also the greatest adventure I have ever gone through. A second chance and a new life. I wanted to be a good steward of my new heart, for sure, but also to *live* every minute of my new life.

This second chance at life has led me to an opened gate and only a hint of a road going through it, very much like the picture that follows. There are no guarantees where the road will lead; in fact, the road itself is likely to get worse the farther we go. The clouds on the mountains in the background portend potential weather problems, too. Much like life itself, the future is unknown. But through that gate is life and lots of it. Maybe sunshine, maybe rain. Problems, likely. Adventure, for sure.

I am going through that gate. Who is with me?

Live well,
Ed

Paige, July 25, 2016

"We must find time to stop and thank the people
who make a difference in our lives."
—JOHN F. KENNEDY

Life is a mystery that has birth and death as bookends. The middle part, all
the stories that compose existence on this earth, are written with each breath
drawn, each heartbeat, and each thought, emotion, and experience. What a
wonder this life is! Opportunities and possibilities present each day as con-
sciousness stirs.

This is a glimpse into part of Ed's story. It is imperfect, incomplete, and
open-ended. Our hope and prayer is that the experiences and thoughts that
are shared will be useful.

There are no warranties or guarantees with a new organ. Other families,
other friends have lost precious loved ones in the past year as Ed has continued to survive and have a new life, a new story, thanks to his donor and the
donor's family. As we are brought to our knees with joy and gratitude, we are

mindful of the grief and loss of others. We weep with them and for them. There is so much sorrow mixed with hope in the transplant story.

No one knows what will happen between the bookends. There is no certainty in tomorrow. Ed's heart is beating today. Now is a gift of unfathomable beauty, sacrifice, and love.

Treasure each day.

Donate Life.

Love and Grace,
Paige Kemper Innerarity

INTRODUCTION

"Life isn't about waiting for the storm to pass . . .
It's about learning to dance in the rain."

—VIVIAN GREENE

Ed

My troubles began on June 14, 2014. Oh, I had known for eight years that I had cardiomyopathy, but the first card of the final hand was dealt that summer day in Colorado.

As was often the case at this time of year, I had my drift boat on the Rio Grande, floating through some of the most beautiful and productive fly-fishing water in the state. The river was still big from the spring runoff, and had I not had a friend in town, I might have waited until the water was down another 1,000 CFS (cubic feet per second) before taking on an eight-mile stretch strewn with foaming rapids and boulders just coming out of hibernation. And besides, I had taken this boat through worse water than this. Just not with a reduced heart function.

Ironically, it was not my heart that was injured that day. Some nerve in my foot, ankle, or leg got overworked as I pushed hard on the foot pegs and pulled hard on the oars to dodge trouble on the Rio Grande. For the next two months, I had limited feeling in that foot and a charley horse in my calf that prevented my cardio workouts that were somehow allowing me to compensate for my heart pumping half the blood it should have.

Cardiomyopathy: Chronic disease of the heart muscle. The heart muscle becomes enlarged, thick, or rigid. As the heart enlarges, it becomes increasingly weaker and unable to pump the blood through the body and maintain a normal heart rhythm. This leads to congestive heart failure.

I got my foot checked out and was told it would take a while for that nerve to regenerate and I would just have to limit my workouts so as not to make Mr. Nerve any madder than he already was. My end-of-summer checkup with my good friend, fellow fly fisherman, and cardiologist, David Terreson, was not as encouraging. I had lost enough conditioning that I had to postpone my September stress test. I was not at all surprised. A couple of weeks before each stress test, I would simulate the Bruce Protocol Stress Test, which I had downloaded from the Internet, on the treadmill at the YMCA. This time I knew I would not do well.

A normal and healthy heart displaces about 55 percent of the blood in the heart chambers and sends it on its way to the lungs and the rest of the body. This is called the ejection fraction, or EF. Shortly after my mother died of congestive heart failure, I got tested as part of an insurance physical. It was then I was first told I had a subnormal EF, the first sign of cardiomyopathy. Having a reduced heart output is like trying to see with half as much light or trying to hear with only half the sound reaching your ear. How well would your car run if only four cylinders of your car's engine were working? I was referred to a cardiologist, Dr. Terreson.

That was in 2006, and my EF was already in the low 40 percent range, but to the doctors' surprise, I was able to function completely. I skied at

11,000 feet; our place in Colorado was at 8,800 feet. I carried my clubs when I played golf, and I had no problem with my cardio workouts. In fact, my first few stress tests were far better than most folks half my age with no heart problems. All of my years of trying to stay fit were allowing me to compensate for my reduced heart function. But regardless of how much I compensated through fitness, there was only so much good it could do.

I was told that with medications and my lifestyle, I might live many more years, but there are no "get out of jail free" cards for cardiomyopathy. The medical statistics say that 15 percent to 20 percent die within one year and another twenty-five percent to 35 percent die within five years.

I was told that this is what I would die of.

At the time, I was fifty-five years old and stood just a hair over six feet tall. I weighed 169 pounds and worked out every day that I didn't play golf, hike, or go to the river. And because of some gene on my mother's side of the family, I was going to die of congestive heart failure. I was careful about what I ate, I was careful about my weight, I did not smoke or drink. But because of some gene, I was going to die. And die ugly.

Sitting with Dr. Terreson in his office, all I could think about was the last six months of my mother's life, or more accurately, the way my mother died for six months. Her hands, legs, and face would swell as she retained fluid. She had no energy, and her skin turned dusky and cold. Her appetite declined and she lost weight. Her voice was weak and raspy. She could hardly walk across the room, even with help. Her eyes were empty save only for the fear and desperation she could not hide. She told me how ready she was to step off that cliff if only she could.

I watched as she suffocated to death because no amount of diuretics and no amount of dobutamine could help keep her lungs from filling with fluid. For sure, hospice staff did a great job trying to make her passing better than it might have been. Less than a year after watching what congestive heart failure looks like wearing my mother's bathrobe, I learned that a bathrobe just like hers had my initials on it.

COUNT YOUR BLESSINGS

In the first few years after World War II, America was tormented and terrorized by polio, aka poliomyelitis, aka infantile paralysis. During this time, the West Texas town of San Angelo reported 420 new cases and twenty-eight polio-related deaths in one year, the highest per capita rate in the country.

In Texas, new cases of polio peaked in 1954, the year the vaccine produced by Jonas Salk was first tested across the country. By August 1955, more than four million Americans had received the polio shot. In my hometown of Midland, a couple of hours northwest of San Angelo, the local paper reported on September 9, 1955, that "the first small shipment of commercial polio vaccine, enough to immunize approximately 100 children, reached Midland this week." The article went on to quote Dr. Dorothy Wyvell, president of the Midland Pediatric Society: "The Midland Pediatric Society anticipates a larger shipment of the serum within the next few months, enough to protect all children by next summer."

Unfortunately for my family, I contracted bulbar polio in October 1955, just before the larger batch of vaccine was due to arrive. It was two weeks short of my fourth birthday. On October 11, 1955, the *Midland Reporter-Telegram* ran a short article, "Two More Midland Children Have Polio; bringing the year's total to 29." The two children were a six-year-old girl named Sandra Duncan and me.

It has taken me many years to realize that my biggest challenges were actually blessings. Having polio as a child was one of them.

My earliest childhood memories were of my bedroom, cleaned out and appearing more like a hospital room. I had a small clinical-type bed, a couple of chairs, and a small stainless-steel table where my injections, spinal tap, blood transfusions, and IV feeding lines were prepared. The same nurse asked me the same question each day: "Ed, what do you want for lunch today?" I always said I wanted a hamburger.

Dr. Wyvell, my pediatrician, would become one of the most influential persons in my life as I got older. I studied economics because of her. After she passed away, I was able to get the original of my medical chart. It noted that I weighed thirty-seven pounds when I got sick, that I had trouble breathing and drooled because I could not swallow. I had lost sensation in my legs and could not move my arms if they were above my head. From my sister I learned that I was not placed in an iron lung because, at my age, my doctor thought the experience would likely be too much for me. So Dr. Wyvell gave me gamma globulin shots made from donated blood plasma to temporarily boost my immune system and prayed for me. I survived. And eventually, I prospered.

The March of Dimes did an unbelievable job raising money and awareness in a warlike effort to defeat polio. Few things tugged at the hearts of postwar Americans more than pictures of young boys and girls in iron lungs or braces, or lying helpless in a hospital. But to be completely honest, many people became infected with polio, felt bad for a few days, and got over it—probably more than 80 percent.

Roosevelt had died barely ten years before, and the images of him in a wheelchair and the posters of pretty young girls in braces were too much for my mother. "My son will not be a cripple," she said more than just a few times. After a few weeks to regain my strength, I was enrolled in tumbling class and was expected to tumble better than the others, which I soon did. "If the seven-year-old boy will walk on his hands, you will too." And I did. "If the eight-year-old boy can learn a back handspring, you will too." And I did. "If the other boy can do a flip on the trampoline, you will too." You will too. You will too.

The things parents say to young children often leave a disproportionately large and permanent mark in the wet cement of that child's life. Looking back, that I survived probably was not the miracle I was told it was. At its worst, in the mid-1950s, polio took three thousand lives in one year, while tuberculosis killed thirty-four thousand people a year at about the same time and influenza caused more than sixty-five thousand yearly deaths. Maybe we should have been looking just as hard at finding a cure for TB and the flu.

Summer could not get to Midland too soon. Finally, a break from vaulting and somersaults. Little did I know that Mother was going to use the swimming pool, the petri dish of polio cultures, to drive all vestiges of weakness from my scrawny legs. I learned to swim so I could swim laps. I was bribed to swim across the pool (cowboy boots). And the length of the pool (a matching hat). And the length and back (a real switchblade knife). By the next summer, at the ripe old age of five, some days I arrived at the pool before the lifeguards. By the end of that summer, I could swim farther and faster than anyone twice my age—in any stroke, underwater or not. How about without taking a breath? That too.

Swim meets logically followed, and diving. It's just tumbling but landing in the water. By the time I burned out completely and found the nerve to tell my mother, I had won state at age fifteen in three-meter diving and could swim any stroke on the high school team. I was giving up something I had done for nearly ten years and had done well. I was part of two Amateur Athletic Union (AAU) relay teams that seldom lost. The AAU promoted various amateur sports, much like the YMCA, and hosted sporting events such as summer swim meets and basketball tournaments. Members of those teams included an All American and a future Olympic gold medal winner. But by now I hated swimming and diving, so I took up tennis instead.

The rehabilitation after polio prepared me for the other obstacles and challenges I would encounter. It also inoculated me against giving up.

More than sixty years later and through the magic of Facebook, I was able to locate Sandra Duncan, the six-year-old who had been diagnosed with polio the same day I was. We were able to visit about our shared experiences. She had a nonparalytic form of polio and recovered. Unlike me, she was confined to the hospital during her illness and recalls seeing a young boy in an iron lung. She had a friend that lived across the alley who also contracted polio and ended up in braces. At the suggestion of Dr. Wyvell, Sandra's mother enrolled her in dance classes, and Sandra went on to be one of the fastest members of the San Jacinto Junior High track team eight years after getting polio.

Every one of us gets polio. OK, not actually polio, but everyone gets their own personal "polio," a major event that forever alters their life trajectory for good or bad. Sometimes it is called drug or alcohol addiction, a broken hip, or cancer. It might be a heart attack, a drunk driver-related auto accident, losing a child, divorce, depression, or domestic violence. Many of these challenges are life changing and often more formidable than what I went through. I am convinced that with each of these personal "polios" comes a chance for rebirth through recovery and the fight to survive—a life lesson for the taking, to be learned if we only will.

I am very blessed to have gone through the polio experience because while it temporarily weakened my muscles, it forever strengthened my resolve. Against all reason and logic, I felt as though my role in life was not to ever give up. If my body had been given a second chance after polio, maybe there was a reason.

Ten years after my skirmish with polio, I was blessed with another life lesson. Instead of a virus, this time it was a future Olympian with an important message for me that would change my life.

In the summer of 1965, a young man named Keith Russell would make a brief but life-altering appearance in my life. He gave me the tools to strengthen my body as well as my resolve, and he was in my life for less than three days.

At the time, Keith was one of the best divers in the county and was hoping to make the US team for the 1968 Mexico City Olympics, which he did. My hometown of Midland was hosting a swim meet and diving exhibition in the summer of 1965, and since I was a young and aspiring diver, it was only right that Keith and another diver would stay at our home during their visit.

I was thirteen years old, and Keith was seventeen or eighteen. I was thin, and he was built like a cross between a world-class gymnast and a modern-day sprinter. He was strong, quiet, and, I learned, a Mormon. I did not know what a Mormon was, except that they were all from Utah, like Oklahomans were Okies or people from Ohio were Buckeyes. Keith was not from Utah, so I guess I knew less about Mormons than I thought. But as I said, I was thirteen.

I observed that before each meal, he returned thanks, and during the meal, he politely passed on coffee, tea, or soda. Later, I asked why. Keith shared with me that he considered his body to be the Lord's temple and how he tried to treat it that way. Over the next few days, he also shared other things directly related to his lifestyle. He was one of the best divers in the world but remained humble. Mind you, these could have been the same things my dad shared with me, but for some reason I listened to Keith. Maybe not so much listened but absorbed.

I never saw Keith again and would have no contact with him over the next fifty years. But I would never forget our conversations, and his impact on my life was profound. Although I burned out on diving within a couple of years of meeting him, I stayed involved in sports and ended up playing tennis in college. In sports and in other parts of my life, I first imitated Keith and then later embraced his lifestyle. I never drank or smoked, although I do enjoy tea. I did not become a Mormon; in fact, Keith and the other diver were the first Mormons I had ever met. But from that first brief encounter, my life was altered forever. Without it feeling like a sacrifice at all, I tried to treat my earthly body as Keith described, a sanctuary for our Heavenly Father. And like Keith, I always tried to stay in shape. To say he made a three-meter-sized mark on my life would be an understatement. I never came close to achieving the athletic success Keith did, but looking back, I got the message.

After my transplant, I was finally able to track Keith down. I wanted to say thanks all these years later and to let him know how meaningful the example he set for me has been and how it helped me prepare for my great medical adventure. It turns out that Keith Russell had just retired after a long and very successful career as head diving coach at Brigham Young University.

Much to my delight, Keith called to talk about the note I sent. Diving was the only thing we did not talk about. He remembered his trip to Midland all those years ago but did not remember me, not that it mattered. He was pleased to hear about my transplant and his small role in the whole big picture. I was able to share with him that my healthy lifestyle gave the doctors many more options. Even with a greatly impaired heart function, I was still able to carry on with life. I skied at altitude, I carried my clubs when I played golf, and I even climbed Half Dome in Yosemite National Park.

As I related earlier, shortly after my mother passed away, I went in for a physical, the kind you get for an insurance policy, and I reminded my family doctor of my mother's heart condition. I passed the insurance part easily, but we decided to do some extra tests to determine if I might have inherited cardiomyopathy from my mother's side of the family.

Let me say right now how much I do not care for hospitals, medical stuff, doctors of any kind, and especially needles and shots. See polio above. I could still remember the spinal taps and blood transfusions. I was just getting a non-invasive echocardiogram, which is nothing more than a sonogram of a beating heart, like they would do on an expectant mother. In rather bad form, the technician asked if I felt OK. Had I been able to walk into the testing room unassisted? Was I having trouble breathing? Looking at me, he saw a normal, healthy-looking guy in his fifties who obviously stayed in shape. But on his computer screen, the technician saw a heart with thickened walls, and the Doppler image revealed a significant reduction in pumping efficiency. I was on the table, but it was my mother's heart on the screen. All that I had learned from swimming, all that I had picked up from Keith, and every other positive life lesson I had absorbed to this point would soon be called upon.

When I was first told what I had, I flinched as if in pain. I had already begun to dismiss what the doctor said. After all, I could work out more, maybe lose a couple of pounds, really watch the salt. Yes, I would will myself through congestive heart failure. This was another swim race, another gymnastics meet, another tennis match; I just needed to want it more than the other guy. After all, that's how I had gotten through life this far; I was never as fast or strong or smart as the others, but if I put my mind to it, I would occasionally find a way to beat some of those guys who were faster, stronger, and smarter. And in my very compartmentalized brain, I gradually accepted a very serious heart condition. The rest of my brain was able to function as before, absolutely sure that nothing was wrong with me. This went on for years because I had taught those different parts of my mind to not discuss important things with each other.

So for the next eight years, I held my own against congestive heart failure. Within a year of my initial diagnosis, Dr. Terreson and an electrophysiologist, Javier Sanchez, decided I needed a defibrillator implanted in my chest in case I was on the river or bird hunting and got an irregular heartbeat, which I did. The device, also called a pacemaker, was designed to gently pace me out of any irregular heart rhythms, and failing that, it could deliver a mighty shock directly to the side of the heart to try and reboot the system. The pacemaker also could communicate, through the skin, to relay information about how my ticker was doing and if the heart needed pacing. I took medications to postpone the inevitable decline in heart function, tried not to dwell on how the end would come, and went about my life. I played golf, I worked at the farm, I fly fished, and I hiked Half Dome. I even had a knee replacement. I lived as though I would not live forever. I learned to sing in the rain since I would not be around by the time the storm clouds passed.

Four months after the incident on the Rio Grande, and not yet back to full strength, I went into atrial fibrillation, afib for short. As in short of breath. As in your life now sucks. As in you feel as though you are trying to breath through a soda straw. As in your car's timing belt just slipped, and your pistons and valves are no longer in sync. Your car may run like that for a while but not long. That was on October 31, 2014. I had played golf that day.

And as they say in the heart business, "Everything is fine until it's not." Now it was not. My getting afib was like having the Mexican peso devalued. Wasn't much there to start with, even less to work with now.

Remember that the defibrillator could talk to other machines through the skin? Each Wednesday at 7 p.m., a small box on my dresser would flash with a small red light, reminding me to "interrogate the device." I would press a couple of buttons on the box, then hold a small corded sensor over the scar where the pacemaker had been implanted. In just under a minute, the box would flash green, meaning the interrogation was over. The quality of every heartbeat since the last interrogation was sent to India or Austin or somewhere and reviewed for signs of trouble.

Just for fun, I would try and hold my breath during the forty-five to fifty-five seconds it took to download the heart data. I had not been told to, and in fact, when the electrophysiologist saw me do so, he was not amused. But it was my way of showing the little box that I was still in charge. And besides, I found the information submitted during the interrogation to be very intrusive. More than once I received a call a couple of days after a download, and the nurse would ask if I was feeling all right. Once in February I got a call saying there was unusual activity around the middle of the month, and was everything OK? The device had recorded increased heart activity the night of Valentine's Day. I was beginning to lose control over my own life. It would get much worse.

Shortly after going into afib, I had my first panic attack/shortness-of-breath episode. I gasped for breath for several minutes before finally being able to breathe normally. I was prescribed an anxiety disorder medication called clonazepam. While it did nothing for the congestive heart failure, it reduced the frequency and magnitude of the panic attacks that came with the seizure-like breathing fits. Soon, I began to look forward to my midday and bedtime visits with clonazepam. I was definitely losing control over my own life.

"Until I feared I would lose it, I never loved to read.
One does not love breathing."

—HARPER LEE, *TO KILL A MOCKINGBIRD*

Six weeks after going into afib, I had to be shocked back into a regular rhythm. Dr. Terreson used paddles on either side of my chest, just like on TV. I was in the hospital for only a couple of days, and except for the two small burn marks, the experience was not too bad. Unfortunately, I continued to decline.

Three weeks after getting shocked, my wife, Paige, and I traveled to Denver to spend Christmas with our ten-month-old granddaughter. Paige and I have been married and partners in this life for more than forty years. When we were teens, we lived just a few blocks apart, and we dated in high school and college. We had raised three beautiful daughters and been through our share of ups and downs together, but now, whether we realized it or not, we were about to face a test neither of us was truly prepared for.

Our granddaughter, Eleanor, weighed sixteen pounds, and I could barely hold her while standing. I had trouble even engaging with my family, and I had serious doubts about walking from the car to church on Christmas Eve. I struggled to walk up the eight steps at the front of the church. I could not function normally, and I had panic attacks just being away from the hotel. Paige thought I was being rude, dramatic, and selfish. I could not predict, control, or rationalize my behavior. I was alone and afraid, even with my family. I stayed alone at the hotel for those few days and wondered if they would find me dead the next morning. Maybe one of those spells of gasping for air would be my last. Maybe Paige was right and I was just being dramatic. But no, I was in advanced congestive heart failure, and Paige was not yet ready to accept that. I was dying. Dying just the same way my mother had.

Forty-four minutes after taking my dose of clonazepam, I would start to come back to life. I would finally warm up after being cold and shivering all day, no matter how many layers of clothes I wore. And one hour and twenty minutes later, I would fall asleep, maybe for the last time. I was never sure. The second night at that hotel by myself in Denver, I prayed as never before. "Lord, if you are going to take me, I am ready. I have had a full life. But please don't let me suffer like this. I can't breathe, I can't breathe. Please do not let me die the way my mother did. Please."

If the trip to Denver was not the bottom for me, it was close. We somehow made it back to Midland, and a day or two later, David Terreson called to say we needed to get to Austin ASAP. The downloaded data from my pacemaker was not good. There were significantly more irregular heartbeats and now from a different part of the heart. The original pacemaker was not designed to handle this new irregular heartbeat. A second pacemaker needed to be implanted immediately. So, on January 1, 2015, in the middle of the worst ice storm to hit Texas in the past twenty-five years, Paige and I spent eight hours driving to Austin. Time to fish or cut bait.

The morning of January 2, 2015, a second pacemaker was implanted and the first one removed. The new one was the latest model with all the latest features for a dead man walking. It had multiple leads, meaning it could pace or shock different parts of the heart. It had a smart chip so advanced that by the time my heart finished a beat, the device was ready to assist on the next beat in a variety of different ways. It did not need to be interrogated as the previous one; it simply found a cell connection and phoned home with any news. ET never phoned home with good news, it was always to report more frequent and longer-lasting irregular heart rhythms. My heart was shaking and shuttering like an old lawnmower started for the first time in the spring. I was now able to feel the arrhythmias (rapid, irregular, or skipped heart beats) as they came more often and lasted longer. The surgery to install the Boston Scientific "HAL 9000" went smoothly enough, but it may have been too little too late. While I was in recovery, the electrophysiologist told Paige that the pacing tests they ran on me while I was out did not go well. The next two weeks would be critical.

The next heap of fun came the day I was to be discharged. I was dressed and ready and did my best to look healthy enough to go home, but the chest x-ray betrayed me. My right lung was full of fluid, and I would have to have it drained. They inserted a very sharp tube into my lung from my back, being very careful not to puncture an artery or hit a rib. I had a good driver, and they got right in, and within thirteen minutes they had drained a liter of fluid. The worst part about the whole thing was the anticipation—I couldn't see what was going on but had plenty of time to amplify in my mind the actual pain that was to come.

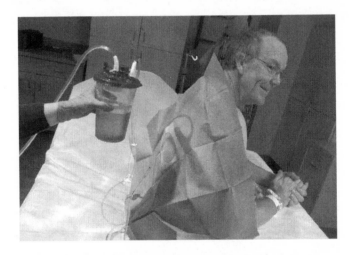

I was released, and the next day we drove back to Midland to rest, recover, and see if the new pacemaker would help me turn the corner. Barely a month later and again betrayed by another chest x-ray, I got the pipe in the back again. Despite taking copious quantities of diuretics and having my fluid intake restricted, they drained two liters of fluid from my right lung, or what looked like two one-liter bottles of turkey broth. I was getting really close to the bottom by now.

I gasped for breath almost constantly, and my liver was more than twice its normal size from being deprived of blood. My gastrointestinal system was not working right because of the lack of the all-important blood supply. My voice was faint and raspy, my arms and legs were atrophied, and I could not walk across the room in the evening. I was very close to giving up.

With all I had been through during my life and all the challenges I was able to work through, I was now ready to quit, give up, and die. Dr. Terreson had run out of tricks and had to turn me over to an end-of-life cardiologist. On March 31, I met with Dr. Mary Beth Cishek.

Not knowing the magnitude and depth of this first meeting, I went alone to Austin. I brought with me my spreadsheet that included my weight, daily dose of diuretics, blood pressure, heart rate, daily exercise, and comments about how I felt and functioned. Dr. Cishek was mildly amused at the spreadsheet, and she wasted little time after the examination in telling me I would not make it to Christmas and that I was dragging myself through life on will alone. One way or another, I needed hospice care, or I could be evaluated for a possible transplant. But I needed to decide soon.

Abbye was a beautiful and special young lady, the same age as one of my daughters, not even thirty years old. Her dad and I had worked together at a now defunct bank thirty years earlier. I would see him around town, and we actually had office space in the same building, but we had very little in common.

Out of the blue one day, he pulled me aside to tell me about his daughter's recent medical diagnosis. I listened intently as he told me her story, so much like mine. Since I was fully compensated and able to function even with significantly reduced heart function, I rarely shared my story beyond my closest friends. So I naturally assumed her dad had learned of what I had and told me about Abbye for that reason. It turns out that her dad did not know I was walking the same path as Abbye. For reasons I would never learn, he just felt the need to tell me about his daughter.

Abbye also had cardiomyopathy. And like me, it developed into acute congestive heart failure. And like me, her best and only option was a heart transplant. But unlike me, her cardiomyopathy and subsequent congestive heart failure progressed very rapidly. Too late, Abbye received the transplant but suffered from bilateral strokes. She lived a heartbreaking, gut-wrenching, soul-consuming two years before passing on. She is now whole, restored, and made perfect again. I was going to die an ugly death within a few months without a transplant. But seeing what happened to Abbye made me fear that even if I somehow qualified for the transplant list, I might be exchanging one set of problems for another.

> "Death is no more than passing from one room into another.
> But there's a difference for me, you know. Because in that other
> room, I shall be able to see."
> —HELEN KELLER

I remember clearly that as soon as my appointment with Dr. Cishek was over, I called to cancel my appointments with my cardiologist and my electrophysiologist. Not much point in having them tell me yet again that I was getting worse. I got into my car and drove north to our farm in Parker County. I had told Paige that after all my appointments, I would drive back to Midland, but I could not.

That night, I had dinner with our middle child, Rebecca, who lives at the farm and has her horse operation there. I asked her what she would do. We talked about the worst that might happen and decided that for me, it was not dying but having a stroke or other complications. I could not help but think of Abbye and every failed transplant story.

It was then that I decided to give the transplant plan a shot, guided by prayer and governed by quality of life. The whole family gathered that Easter weekend at the farm to celebrate the possibility of my making the transplant list. No guarantees, to be sure. Lots of hospital time and lots of uncomfortable tests just to make sure that I might be a worthy and suitable steward for a donated heart. Then possibly would come a transplant operation with all that entails and then a long and potentially arduous recovery.

Every family of a prospective transplant recipient faces problems and factors unique to that case. Those families' hopes and fears are as important as they are different from mine. No words of mine are needed to validate the way any family approaches a possible transplant or the inevitable problems that come with that procedure. They are as unique as the hearts that are donated by the grieving families. As for me, I was also finally able to deal with the stroke issue. With Paige's complete support, I decided that life after a devastating stroke would not be really living. If I did have a stroke, I would not be kept alive because of a medical directive to be bedridden and a burden to everyone. Nope, either I would live or I would die.

After the weekend with my family, I returned to Midland for a few days to update my will and get my affairs in order. Barely a week after meeting Mary Beth Cishek, I was ready to turn my life over to her and the transplant team. I was about to embark on the greatest adventure of my life.

Most of what follows are the emails I sent to my family and friends while being evaluated for possible listing on the transplant waiting list, while on the list hoping a matching heart would be found in time, and while recovering from the surgery. Many were written while I was in ICU before a procedure, during the transplant evaluation, or after a biopsy or other test.

"They say you die twice. One time when you stop breathing and a second time, a bit later on, when someone says your name for the last time."

—BANKSY

"Never believe that you know the last word about any human heart."

—HENRY JAMES

Paige

Greg Louganis, the incredible American diver who excelled at both spring-board and platform diving, won forty-seven national and thirteen international championships, including four gold medals and one silver at the Olympics. Ed and I were watching a TV interview during the Montreal Olympics, and Greg was asked if platform diving was "like flying." He smiled that beautiful smile and said, "No, it is falling, and it is terrifying." I looked at Ed, and he said, "Yes! It is absolutely terrifying. I was scared every single time I was up there."

Now, Ed is the same guy I have watched do daredevil dives from cliffs into lakes and bridges into rivers, and flips off the one-meter board with one of our toddlers held to his chest. He has ridden dirt bikes over mountain passes on old mining roads, climbed mountains, taken his fishing boat down rivers that were risky, surfed and swum in dangerous currents, and gotten lost in the wilderness on solo backpack trips. The number of times he has gotten a hunting vehicle stuck or been broken down somewhere in a blizzard or ice storm is too many to count. In spite of the risks he took, and this is only a representative sampling, the children and I never really worried about him. Ed is very resourceful, incredibly self-reliant, and has a MacGyver-like talent for problem-solving. But even Superman has a weakness. Cardiomyopathy was Ed's kryptonite.

By Christmas 2014, Ed was falling off the cliff from a medical stand-point. All the drugs that had kept his cardiomyopathy at bay could no longer keep his heart pumping enough to sustain him. Walking across the room left him gasping for breath, he was having full-blown panic attacks because he was in pain and exhausted. Nights were terrible. He was terrified of not waking up while, at the same time, saying he wanted to die and "not have to hurt anymore and be so scared." Ed and I had promised our Colorado daughters, Laura Paige and Sarah, that we would drive to Denver to celebrate Christmas there. It would be the first Christmas for our granddaughter, Eleanor, Laura Paige's daughter. Sarah, our oldest daughter, and Cameron, her soon-to-be fiancé, would drive over Christmas Day from Glenwood Springs to be with everybody in Denver. Cameron got sick right before they left, so he didn't make the trip. Cameron had the best Christmas of all of us, and he had the flu!

Our stay in Denver was brief, which was fortunate. Ed was feeling worse every day. All I could think of was that we needed to get back to Texas—Austin, specifically, where his doctors were. Surely, there was something that could be done to kick-start his cardiovascular system, his ability to breathe? I had not yet learned that heart disease can be managed beautifully for years, until the day arrives when everything goes terribly wrong.

Before Ed even was aware that he had cardiomyopathy, his lifestyle was what all cardiologists want for their patients: he didn't smoke, he didn't drink, he exercised faithfully. These were conscious choices, which he made from a very young age. Having polio as a child and being physically weak, he worked to build up his strength and stamina. Being a competitive swimmer and diver, he encountered elite athletes, such as Keith Russell, who inspired him and instilled in him the desire to treat his body respectfully, as a gift from God. Not many thirteen-year-old boys carry through the lifetime habits that Ed had cultivated. The fact that he did make these choices, and had the tenacity of a bull terrier, meant he was the ultimate underdog/overachiever.

No wonder it was such a sobering and truly unbelievable fact for our friends, family, and me to accept that Ed, virtually within a few days, could not walk five yards without gasping for breath. I cannot imagine anything more terrifying than being unable to draw a full breath, to feel the same sort of panic one feels being held underwater and only allowed little sips of air before being forced to submerge again.

We headed to Austin as soon as we could schedule appointments. In early December, a procedure to "shock" Ed's heart back into a normal rhythm worked, but his heart was increasingly overburdened by its inability to pump efficiently, which led to fluid collecting around his lungs, which led to more problems breathing.

A new pacemaker, with all the latest bells and whistles, was installed but to no avail. Having the electrophysiologist, Dr. Javier Sanchez, whom we had known for six years, say to me after the surgery, "The next two weeks will make it apparent if it is going to help, but, Paige, I am not optimistic," left me dazed and distraught. So I gave my emotions free rein, cried in the blessedly empty waiting room for twenty minutes, and then washed my face and composed myself before Ed was out of recovery. This could not be happening! Were we really at the end of the line?

A procedure was done a couple of times over about a two-month period. I would sit next to the examining table where Ed was perched and watch the tech administer a local anesthetic with a tiny needle into Ed's back and then stick a large hollow needle through to siphon off straw-colored fluid. The men and women who did this procedure were unfailingly kind, gentle, and very good at their job. We had wonderful conversations with them, about their work, about their lives and ours. We had questions, we had concerns. We were on a quest to obtain as much information as we could from the folks who were on the front lines in the battle to restore Ed's health.

With very few exceptions, the medical folks we encountered were patient, knowledgeable, and willing to educate us. To this day, we are so grateful for this knowledge exchange. It kept us focused, it allayed our fears, and it helped us to be realistic as the weeks and months continued to prove that Ed's heart was not going to sustain his life. I have to give Ed a great deal of credit for his attitude during the fluid-drawing procedure. For a man who had developed a fear of needles from being poked for blood draws and IVs daily when he was a tiny boy with polio, Ed took this procedure amazingly well. The first time this fluid was drained, it filled a bottle to the one-liter mark. Only a few weeks later, two liters of fluid were siphoned from around Ed's lungs. Sadly, the progression of Ed's heart disease was picking up steam.

It was not long after that, maybe three weeks, when David Terreson had "The Talk" with Ed.

Being Ed's cardiologist, fishing buddy, and close friend (not necessarily in that order) gave David insight and access to Ed's thoughts and feelings on a deeper level than was usual in the relationship between a doctor and his patient. Of course, I do not want to discount Dr. Terreson's ability to relate to all his patients, because he has a wonderful ability to communicate that cannot be overstated. The fact was that Dr. Terreson needed every advantage to convince Ed to take a step, actually a leap, in treatment. Gently, solemnly, David told my husband that there was nothing else he could do for him. "Ed, we have had a great run for eight years. You have been an awesome and compliant patient, doing everything you could to take care of yourself and your heart, but there is nothing else I can do for you. I really want to send you to see Dr. Mary Beth Cishek at Seton Transplant Center. I know you have always said you would not get a transplant under any conditions. Please, just make an appointment to see her. She might have some ideas of medications that I'm not aware of, or procedures that can help you. Just go talk to her."

What could Ed say? Despite having no intention whatsoever of even considering a transplant, Ed agreed to see Dr. Cishek. In numerous conversations with our children; my brother, Jim; my sister, Caroline; his closest friends; and with me, Ed had repeatedly and unequivocally stated that he would not put himself or his family through a transplant. He believed, and rightly so, that his life had been richly blessed, full of adventures, challenges, and triumphs. He knew of no other person who had as few regrets or as many wonderful experiences. The inherent risks, assuming he even lived long enough to receive a new heart, terrified him. The very real possibility of being mentally and physically incapacitated after the surgery was not a chance he was willing to take, for himself or his loved ones. End. Of. Discussion. This was a debate with no rebuttal.

All of us who loved Ed knew that this was a decision that was his alone. There were no guarantees, no statistics that would support any argument. Everything that he thought, every fact supported his thesis. If he was not willing to go through the transplant process, which, honestly, no one knew if he would even be accepted to attempt, that was his decision. Life, at this point, was rapidly losing its quality. The possibility of life and the certainty of death, the ability to choose rested in his hands and his alone. We all loved and respected Ed too much to do anything but honor his choice. His heart might be worn out and failing him, but we would be with him, regardless of our grief and his choice. Of course, this was before Ed's appointment with Dr. Mary Beth Cishek. No one could have predicted how *that* would turn out.

It was the Tuesday before Easter. Our daughter Rebecca has a horse farm near Weatherford, Texas. Our other daughters, future son-in-law, and granddaughter were all meeting there for another attempt at a happy holiday gathering after the Christmas debacle in Denver. We were determined to make this a joyous, spiritual time for Ed's sake, for baby Eleanor's sake, and for all of us. It was to be a celebration of life, of faith, of family, regardless of the circumstances we were facing. Ed was in Austin, seeing Dr. Cishek for what I assumed would be one appointment only. I stayed in Midland to pack up clothes, food, boxes of diapers, a car seat, a pack-and-play, and so on. Ed would meet me at the farm the following afternoon after an appointment with David Terreson. I was hopeful that we could all be together and celebrate Easter. It was 1:30 p.m., and I had just left my Tuesday Bible study when my phone rang as I got in the car. I saw that it was Ed. "Hey, Ed, how was your appointment?"

Ed: (in a very subdued voice) "Uh, well, I am still here. I am with Dr. Cishek. She wants to talk to you."

Me: "Oh, OK, did you explain why I wasn't with you? That I was scrambling to get everything together for the weekend?"

Ed: "Oh, yes, I did. She understood perfectly. Paige, did you know I am dying?"

Me: "Well, yes, Ed, I did know that."

Ed: "Really? How did you know? Who else knows? Did you know I will be dead by Christmas if I don't get a heart transplant?"

Me: "Let's see . . . the children all know. Caroline and Jim know. Mary Beth [different Mary Beth—our practically family friend and minister] and Jeff [the different Mary Beth's husband, our lawyer, and ditto in the friendship category] know. David Koch knows, and Barbara, because you and I told them. Ed, I did not know a specific time line, but I am not surprised at Dr. Cishek's prognosis. Are you surprised?"

Ed: "I guess I am surprised it is so soon. Dr. Cishek says I have two choices. I can be evaluated to see if I am a candidate for a transplant, or I can go into palliative care. Do you know what that is?"

Me: "Hospice."

Ed: "Yes. Hospice. There is nothing to be done for me unless I get a new heart. No medicine, no therapy, no procedure. This is it. She wants to talk to you."

Dr. Cishek: "Mrs. Innerarity, were you aware that your husband is dying? He is dragging himself through life."

Me: "Yes, Dr. Cishek. Please call me Paige. Our whole family is painfully aware he is dying. He has been told by Dr. Sanchez and Dr. Terreson that there is nothing else they can do for him. For some reason, it did not seem to register until he saw you that he really is dying."

Dr. Cishek: "Paige, if I had my way, I would admit him to the hospital right now. He is in terrible shape, and there is no time to waste. He needs to be evaluated for the transplant program, which takes a week, at least. There are no guarantees he will even qualify for the program, but we need to see and try to get him on the transplant list as soon as possible. I understand you are spending Easter at the farm with your children. This will give you all a chance to talk about this decision. I want him back here as soon as you both can be here, for an indefinite stay. I will let you speak with Ed."

Ed: "Soooo . . . that was Dr. Cishek. I will call you after I leave here."

Me: "Ed, are you going to get evaluated for a heart transplant?"

Ed: "Yes, I am. I don't want to be dead by Christmas. I will call you in a bit. Love you."

Sometimes, it just takes the right messenger delivering the news. I bless Mary Beth Cishek from the top of her head to the soles of her feet every single day for being that messenger. She delivered the news of Ed's imminent demise with an authority and candor that was akin to being smacked with a two-by-four. He heard her, loud and clear. The "Sweet By and By" now had a date attached to it, and Ed was not ready to "go quietly into that good night." Hallelujah and pass the ammunition! Ed was in for the fight of his life, the adventure to top anything he had experienced in a lifetime of amazing adventures and blessings beyond either of our wildest imaginings.

It was the best Easter our family has ever had.

But, after Easter, there was a tremendous shift in our lives. Once Ed had committed to being evaluated as a transplant candidate, our whole family pushed all our chips to the center of the poker table. We were "all-in," individually and collectively. Our friends added their emotional and spiritual collateral, and our stack of chips grew. Even though we had yet to meet the medical professionals who would become an integral part of Ed's and my life, they were already on board, whether they knew it or not. Transplant professionals, at least the ones we know, are engaged one-hundred-percent with taking care of patients. The doctors, nurses, technicians, physical therapists, psychologists, social workers, pharmacists, and everyone else who streamed into our lives gave their attention, considerable training, and expertise to helping Ed stay alive long enough to receive a heart. Little did we know that many of these folks would become a permanent part of our lives. The bonds formed are unbreakable, because our appreciation is profound.

The race against time that is the cornerstone of cardiomyopathy began when Ed walked into Seton Hospital for a week of testing. The relationships with fellow patients, their families, and health-care providers are forever. Ed and I learned that putting our trust in the hands of others to save his life was required. At the same time, we were not willing to count on strangers to be caregivers; we just are not "wired" that way. Strangers became acquaintances and, in many cases, have become our friends.

The emails and narrative Ed and I have cobbled together is a scrapbook of sorts. It includes some medical information and lots of stories and anecdotes that helped us cope as we navigated heart disease: the fears, the questions, the tender mercies, and the miracles of every day as a transplant patient. Our hope and prayer is that those who are still experiencing The Waiting are not doing so in vain. Organ donation is so simple, so beautiful, so critical to saving lives. If you get nothing else from flipping through these pages, our goal is accomplished: Be a good steward of this one life you have, and pass it on through organ donation.

> "If we were logical, the future would be bleak indeed.
> But we are more than logical. We are human beings,
> and we have faith, and we have hope, and we can work."
> —JACQUES COUSTEAU

PART 1

Landslide

"I don't know where I'm going, but I'm on my way."
—CARL SANDBURG

Heraclitus of Ephesus lived awhile back, around 500 BC, according to those who study ancient philosophers. He is called "the dark philosopher" because his writings are considered to be difficult to understand. My research also revealed that Heraclitus had a very high opinion of his own work, considering himself to be the only philosopher of his time. He is best known for stating, "The only constant in life is change." Now, I may not have been the deepest thinker in my high school History of Western Civilization class, but that concept has stuck with me throughout my life and empirically proven itself.

When Ed decided he wanted to be evaluated for the transplant program, our life changed immediately. I drove home from Bible study, parked my car in the garage, put on my old straw hat and walking shoes, and headed out for a walk through the neighborhood. Walking is the way I center myself and clear my mind. I know yoga is supposed to put one in a meditative state, but try as I might, as I crouch in a child's pose or creakily assume downward dog, I have never achieved anything but a state involving making lists, wondering how much longer I have to do this pose, and debating if I have time to pick up the dry cleaning after class. Perhaps I have a bad attitude, but walking calms me. It allows me to let go of my cares, and the chattering of my brain disappears. Ideally, the walk involves mountains and a creek or river alongside the trail. In a pinch, any sidewalk will suffice. After an hour walking the neighborhood, I was ready to jump into the changes and transitions that were approaching like an avalanche. Thank goodness I was blissfully unaware of how drastic those changes would be.

I have always considered myself to be pretty adaptable in the face of change. Like most people, I have faced adversity at various stages in my life. Physical challenges after a wreck that left my body broken and led to twelve surgeries in two years was pretty daunting. I was blessed to have had great medical care and amazing friends and family to put me back together, physically and emotionally. I grew spiritually and have never felt more loved and connected to my Creator, but this was not the landslide I experienced watching Ed face a future that was fraught with peril. It is always easier to go through dangerous waters than to watch someone you love suffer and struggle. As the Fleetwood Mac song said, I had built my life around someone, and seeing the changes that were coming forced me to be bolder—whether I was ready or not. We both needed to let the child in our heart, who had faith, help us rise above the fear and move forward.

The first change we faced was a week of tests and interviews at Seton to see if Ed qualified for a transplant. Ed had the tests and procedures; we both had the interviews. My amazing sister, Caroline, showed up the fourth day and stayed until Ed received the news that he was on the list. By then, another change had occurred. My childhood friend, Francie Little, who is a real estate broker in Austin, helped me locate a furnished apartment one block from the hospital. I signed the month-to-month lease before Ed was even released from his weeklong evaluation. We moved in the next day. Our new life had begun.

That new life became centered around preparing Ed to become the best possible recipient and steward of his new heart. We could not allow ourselves to dwell too much on the only other possibility, but it was always lurking, unbidden and unwelcome, in the back of our minds. I believe all potential organ recipients are cognizant of the race they are running. It is a race against terrible odds. The clock is ticking relentlessly as the warranty is running out on one or more organs. Prospective recipients work incessantly to keep their bodies going long enough for an organ donation. Family and friends are praying, exhorting, and cheering from the sidelines, but it is a lonely race, no matter how encouraging the fans try to be. Being scrutinized daily by doctors, nurses, physical therapists, and family is nerve-racking and exhausting. Looking back, and knowing Ed's desire for peace, privacy, and normalcy, I cannot believe how well he coped. He had gone from living a very independent life to being hooked up to a milrinone infusion pump twenty-four seven in a tiny apartment, with me in his face almost every minute of the day. Of course, he had breaks from me when he rode his bike to the hospital to be questioned, poked, prodded, and evaluated at physical therapy. Yes, our life had changed dramatically.

Milrinone: A drug used for the short-term treatment of heart failure. It works by making your heart beat stronger and by dilating certain blood vessels so that the amount of blood that is pumped from the heart is increased. This effect may help with symptoms of heart failure.

Perhaps the most unexpected change was our desire to withdraw from most social interaction. For us, it seemed that every day involved hospital appointments, phone calls, and time spent learning more information relating to new prescriptions, new therapies, and changes in Ed's treatment. Communicating with all of the wonderful people who loved us was virtually impossible and, frankly, would have been emotionally exhausting. The idea for the emails was born out of necessity, as emotional and physical collateral were in very short supply. It was cathartic for Ed to write his thoughts about the changes in his life, and I enjoyed writing my perspective as well. This became a way for us to keep in touch while withdrawing, temporarily, from our tribe. Honestly, we were on a quest that required leaving our people and concentrating on a goal. Ed was the Lone Ranger and I was Tonto.

As Ed worked to stay alive long enough to get a heart, I worked, not terribly successfully, to find something he could eat. For some reason that was never really determined, all food tasted terrible. Ed had a horrific taste in his mouth, possibly related to medication or to physiological changes occurring as his body fought to keep going; we never knew for sure. Food was a huge problem. I have always prided myself on preparing nutritious and tasty meals, and Ed has always had a great appetite and appreciated my efforts in the kitchen. No matter what I cooked, no matter what he ordered in restaurants, he had no appetite, and everything had a metallic taste. Dr. Cishek brought a sack full of liquid nutritional supplements to the hospital the last day of Ed's evaluation for him to sample. None of them were palatable. Finally, through trial and error, I found one he could choke down. He would drink three to four of them a day, eat as much as he could (which was not too much), and continue to lose weight. Ed normally weighs 170 pounds; by the day of his transplant, he weighed 145 pounds. Less than what he weighed going into college. To me, it was a frightening change in my normally robust and fit six-foot husband.

Adapting to change is essential if we don't want to go the way of the dinosaur. Being flexible or altering the course in the midst of life's turbulence demands attention to detail, intuition, ability to rethink and reorder priorities, sensitivity to changing surroundings, and more than a little luck. We know we have been incredibly fortunate in every measure of life's circumstances. Through a series of events, we ended up in Austin, at Seton Transplant Center. The people encountered leading up to Ed's decision to be evaluated as a transplant candidate were the perfect people to lead him to that decision. Our friends and family who supported us during the seemingly endless changes leading up to the transplant were exactly who we needed. Change is difficult, uncertainty is uncomfortable, and both must be confronted by everyone who draws breath. We are humbled and amazed by the guidance, divine and mortal, that we received as we faced constant change.

"I'd just as soon kiss a Wookiee."

—PRINCESS LEIA

From: Ed Innerarity
Sent: Wednesday, April 8, 2015 9:22 PM
Subject: DAY ONE

Dear Angels and Armorers,

Somewhere in the Bible, there is listed all the armor of God we are to wear: the belt of truth, the gospel of peace, the shield of faith, the helmet of salvation, and the sword of the Spirit. In your own way, I believe that each of you, and others, has handed me the various pieces of that armor, plus I like the analogy of getting ready for battle, because I am in for the fight of my life. With no guarantees about the outcome, only faith that I fight the best battle possible.

That being said, I may simply refer to you as my Armorers.

We got a call first this a.m. asking for us to come a day early, so we drove like mad and got to the Seton Heart Institute about 2:30. I was immediately whisked to the back for multiple blood draws coming out of both arms. My BP was too low to fill all 19 Gatorade bottles so they were squeezing my arms and having me pump my fists. Half an hour later, Erin had his blood and the tests began. Test #1, what is my blood type; pretty much a big deal statistically in improving my odds. I will be tested for blood type on more than one occasion with different labs doing independent reports. The next two hours were full of intense counsel and innumerable releases all with a lengthy explanation of risk. Had Paige not been with me, I am not sure I would have been able to remain upright. I was fighting a major anxiety attack and losing badly. By the time it was over, I was unexplainably cold, shaking uncontrollably, and barely able to speak. We finally made it to the hotel and headed off to dinner. I am sorry to report the panic attack was just getting going, but we finally made it to the room and I took a hot shower that lasted so long, the Comanche Peak Nuclear Power Plant in Glen Rose was working overtime.

Much better now and ready for tomorrow which includes sunrise surgery to insert a narrow and fairly clean, flexible coat hanger into my vein in my neck, swing south below the heart then mosey back over to the right side of the heart to say "hello, how ya' doing?" That stays in for a couple of days while I get the royal spa treatment in ICU.

DAY ONE SCORE: **Seton Heart Institute 21, Ed 3**

I avoided the shut out today with a late field goal only because they really like Paige, and I otherwise fit the profile for a good transplant recipient: not overweight, never smoked, not diabetic, about the right size, likely to do all the post-op stuff. Fracking and golfing were not held against me.

There is still no guarantee that I will make the list, where I might be placed on the list, or if a suitable heart will be found in time, which gets me back to the shield of faith.

May be off the grid for a couple of days while in ICU.

Still plenty of time to narrow the score.

ed

From: Rebecca Innerarity
Sent: Wednesday, April 8, 2015 9:31 PM
Subject: Re: DAY ONE

"Because he loves me," says the Lord. "I will rescue him; I will protect him, for he acknowledges my name. He will call upon me, and I will answer him; I will be with him in trouble, I will deliver him and honor him."

—Psalm 91:14-15

From: Sarah Innerarity
Sent: Wednesday, April 8, 2015 9:41 PM
Subject: Re: DAY ONE

Praying & sending every bit of love, hope & strength your way!

Get some rest tonight & I'm sure you'll even the score over the next couple days & win in a tiebreaker in the third set with a ripping cross-court forehand (even though those are two different sports).

Many more fish to catch, sunsets to see, brownies to eat, and fun times to be had.

Love you,
Sass

From: Paige Innerarity
Sent: Wednesday, April 8, 2015 10:10 PM
Subject: News from Austin

Dear Precious Friends,

Ed and I are finally settled at the hotel in Austin and have a very early wake-up call to be at Seton Heart Institute at 5:30. As all of you know, Ed's cardiomyopathy took a dramatic turn on November 1st when he went into afib. I will not get into the gory details, but numerous trips to Austin since then, including several lengthy hospital stays and procedures, have not been successful in reversing the downward turn in his cardiac health. As David Terreson, Ed's cardiologist and dear friend has said, Ed had incredible compensation for eight years, the best he has ever seen, but he has finally used up his hall pass and it is time for a new heart.

We met with the congestive heart failure/cardiac staff today for two hours for a crash course in what to expect for the next 4–5 days. Ed will have a right heart catheterization tomorrow to measure his internal heart pressures, tweak IV meds, monitor how his heart responds to said meds, etc., etc., and so forth. He will spend at least one night in ICU, then be moved to the third floor for more tests. We should be leaving the hospital Monday or Tuesday. During this time, we will be meeting with thoracic surgeons, a psychologist, pulmonary specialist, social worker, and the five people we spent the afternoon with in Mary Beth's office. Oh! Mary Beth is the doctor in charge of Ed for the rest of his life, and she is amazing. So, with two Mary Beths helping us sort out the spiritual and physical aspects of our lives, we should be in good hands.

Honestly, this is all completely overwhelming. I am closing with very specific prayer requests.

1. Pray that Ed passes all the tests to be accepted on the transplant list. This is not a slam-dunk. He needs to meet very specific criteria to be considered for the list, and then voted onto the list by the doctors and staff who are involved in the program. The meeting and the vote take place on Wednesday.

2. Pray for a spot near the top of the list. Time is of the essence. Fifty percent of patients on the transplant list do not live long enough to receive a heart.

3. Pray for Ed to have peace, a calm spirit, and a positive attitude. His body and emotions have taken a terrible battering since November 1st. He is the finest and bravest man I have ever known, and I hate to watch the toll this is taking.

4. Pray for our family. Our children have all stepped up in a mighty way and I could not be more grateful for the part each one has played in supporting and loving us. Sarah, Rebecca, Laura Paige, Brian, and Baron have been amazing, and I love them more than I can ever say. My sister, Caroline, my brother, Jim, and their families keep us in the fight.

5. Pray for the doctors, nurses, technicians, and everyone else at Seton who will be taking care of my darling Ed. Everyone we have met exhibits professionalism and concern. We are grateful to them all. I would be remiss if I did not mention the love, friendship, and incredible care Ed has received from David Terreson and Javier Sanchez over the last eight years. They are extraordinary cardiologists and exemplify the very best of what medicine should be.

6. Thank you for loving us. We love you all for standing in the gap for us.

Love and Grace,
Paige

From: Ed Innerarity
Sent: Thursday, April 9, 2015 10:07 PM
Subject: DAY TWO

"How did it get so late so soon?"

—DR. SEUSS

Today started at 4:30 a.m. in order to be at the hospital at 5:30 a.m. for the fun to begin. Admitted and moved into pre-op in military fashion. I had the really clean coat hanger inserted in my neck to check pressures on the right side of my heart. BUT, not before the ports were inserted and more blood was spilled than at Bull Run. I was kept awake during the procedure to ensure the most accurate reading possible. I was draped and face covered but could hear the team at work. The coat hanger has a pressure-measuring device at the end, which was inserted 61 cm into scared & shaking Eddie. The goal was to have that pressure-measuring device located right in the pulmonary artery. As far as I could tell, it was in there just right, so I was taken by gurney to ICU. Little did I know that breezy, dopey ride on the gurney would be one of the three highlights of my day.

Wasting not one minute, blood was drawn six different times to test for everything I have ever heard of. If I had ever traveled to Arkansas, one of the tests showed that. Details of post-polio syndrome and my lung health were examined in great detail including a fresh chest x-ray. Probable fluid there will be dealt with later. Faxes were traded with my dentist and primary care doctor. Any test, vaccine, or immunization that was not current or verifiable will be repeated. TB test next. Then clot buster shots into the belly for good measure.

A quick walk around the hall to make sure the hospital gown is in fact two sizes too small. A hearty breakfast at 10:30 a.m. A colonoscopy was added to the list for day after tomorrow, so I am out for golf on Saturday. Detailed interview with the pulmonologist. All going well so far; nothing particularly fun but I am passing the various hurdles and have not been disqualified by anything yet. An oxygen artery test turned out to eat my lunch. The unhappy pain face on the wall was beginning to look like me. Then, I am told the right arm did not work so we needed to try the other arm "if I didn't mind." Happy to accommodate except that I had torn holes in the sheet and mattress "remaining calm and relaxed." I earned no points by comparing the pain to natural childbirth.

Now lunch time, but no lunch until the colonoscopy details are confirmed. The decision was made to prep me over two days instead of one to spare me the potential fluid overload. Anyway, who wouldn't want to drink the Go Quickly for 48 hours? So, clear fluids it is until Mr. C comes to visit. So, I wonder if anyone else has ever had a colonoscopy with the coat hanger thing in their neck.

I played the "dead man walking" card and traded several pain killers to the guys in the basement to come up and hardwire my TV so I could get the Masters coverage. The second highlight of my day was being able to watch the Masters during injections and blood draws. More interviews, social workers, physical therapist, rehab people, thoracic surgeon (who might perform any transplant), flight coordinators, dietician,

GI people, all with clipboards filled with places for check marks or big Xs. Kind of like a parole board, not sure how they want things answered. Seriously, I am aware a new heart will only become available because someone's dad or brother or son loses his life. I think about that a lot.

My RN, Yonus, rotated off at 7:00 p.m., and just before he left, I asked if we knew yet what my blood type was. Yonus looks like someone who had fished with Peter and John. Yonus walked in without saying a word, gave me the thumbs up with a big smile like he had just cast his net on the other side of the boat. I knew what he was telling me: I am A positive! To call it the third highlight of the day would be a huge understatement. Being A+ significantly improves the odds that they might find a matching heart. While I am far from being out of the woods, this news could easily make the difference in living and dying. I cried. Paige was just walking in the room, and I told her that I felt more than ever that I was going to live. Again, lots of pieces need to fall into place.

DAY TWO SCORE: **Seton Heart Institute 28, Ed 12.** (Box score would show I got a touchdown with the interview with the actual surgeon, a field goal with the gurney ride, and two points for a safety. I am counting the blood type news as the safety. Every team will tell you that a safety is always worth more than just the two points, and it frequently is a momentum changer.)

[*Song #1*. Attached to this email was a link to "Slip Slidin' Away" by Paul Simon. Certain emails that I sent along this journey contained links to a song or songs I wanted my family and friends to listen to before, during, or after reading the email that day. These songs helped get across emotions or thoughts that I couldn't put into words at the time. I have included notes like this throughout to indicate when a song was included with an email so readers can listen along as well.]

From: Paige Innerarity
Sent: Thursday, April 9, 2015 10:09 PM
Subject: Heart Evaluation 101, Or How We Are Spending Our Summer
Vacation

Dear Ones,

When Ed and I woke up at 4:30 this morning to prepare to go to the
hospital, neither of us could have imagined what this day would hold for
us. It has been intense, emotional, and affirming from beginning to end.
We have spent virtually every minute since Ed was wheeled into ICU
after his right heart catheterization talking and listening to a revolving
cast of doctors, nurses, and techs. My brain is exploding with all the
information we have received. My heart is overflowing with all the care
and concern we have received. My spirit is soaring with all the prayers
that have protected and lifted us throughout this day.

Without exception, every person we have met has been kind, gen-
uinely concerned, and invested in Ed's case. So far, all of the test results
indicate he would be a candidate for a transplant. We learned this evening that his blood type is "A positive"—a huge advantage for a prospective transplant recipient. So far, every test that has been administered is
further proof that he is likely to be admitted to the transplant list.

Tomorrow, there will be more tests, more interviews, more information for us to absorb and retain. Please continue to pray for Ed to have
the fortitude, attitude, and mindset to continue to meet the challenges
he faces. We are convinced that we are in the right place, surrounded by
the right people with the right skills to give Ed his life back. Thank you

all for your prayers and encouragement. We are overwhelmed by your love and it gives us the strength to put one foot in front of the other when the burden seems to be unbearable.

Love and Grace,
Paige

From: Ed Innerarity
Sent: Saturday, April 11, 2015 7:15 AM
Subject: DAY THREE

> "I learned that courage is not the
> absence of fear, but the triumph over it."
> —NELSON MANDELA

Today kind of took its toll, so I am not writing this until early the next morning.

I was struck by a couple of things: how poorly my earplugs work at night and how ironic it is that they keep wanting to have a serious discussion about me increasing my calorie input but continue to have me on clear liquids only since I got here.

Life-saving IV meds caused me to have a blinding headache most of the day so I was not really able to write. Staff consistently and nearly uniformly professional and available. I am not sure if I have just ignored it, been lucky, or am now really coming to terms with how advanced my cardiac problems are. So much so that I am probably here at the hospital until something is resolved; either something is discovered that keeps me off the list, or I make the list with a high priority number and see if I can make it until a heart becomes available.

I had a non-invasive echocardiogram; heart output continues to decline, approaching single digits. It still gets to them that I am able to do my walks without much effort. They cannot figure out where that is coming from. I tried to explain about my armorers, and they thought I was just getting light-headed.

Having a colonoscopy in a few hours and the prep was spread out over 24 hours to not overload my system. I was also moved to a new larger ICU room where about every procedure is performed, including the colon blow. New room meant that the new TV did not have the digital package set up and no Masters. "Dead man walking" card played again with the guys from maintenance and, voila, the dogwoods and azaleas are back. Something curious about doing a daylong colonoscopy prep with the whispering voices they use during the Masters coverage. I was promised a steak as soon as the colon camera is out. By the way, try going through the prep process with a portable toilet behind a small sheet of cheesecloth at DFW airport Concourse C and you get the amount of privacy I had. Not to mention all the wires and tubes I am still connected to.

An EKG and several more blood profiles. I am pretty sure they have all the blood they need but are doing the extra blood draws just to make sure I am still "all in." More interviews, psychologist, pulmonologist, head transplant guru, even the chaplain showed up, a very nice young Baptist minister who does his work at the hospital. Speaking of which, I was asked by a couple of the staff about my "religion" and did I turn to my religion now under the circumstances. I told them I was a Christian and a believer but that I thought of my faith more like the primer sprayed on my car before it was painted. It's there, it has always been there, maybe not visible under the shiny coats of paint applied later, but it's there for sunny days or rain to be depended on in good times or tough. Not sure they understood. Not sure which of you handed me my shield of faith, coat of primer, but you will understand.

Later in the day, the big cheese transplant doctor, Mary Beth, and the chief pulmonologist sat us down for a serious discussion of a heart lung machine as a temporary worst-case resuscitation option. Something we needed to hear now so that a quick decision could be made if something serious happened. Even after all of this time and the acuteness of my situation, it is hard to hear myself speaking in normal sentences about such things. Paige will make the right call if something comes up. During that conversation, I was becoming aware that certain doctors at Seton are pushing hard for me to make the Wednesday transplant list; in fact, I may be qualified as early as Monday if this morning's drive through the colon goes well. I must credit Paige for a fair share of that, as they seem taken with her. Another big hurdle to pass today is the upper and lower GI tract inspection. As they said, they need the heart to go to the healthiest host possible, consistent with need.

I am not able to respond to your many wonderful emails, and I am generally worn out by all the testing, but it does not mean I don't appreciate it.

DAY THREE SCORE: **Seton 10, Ed 10** (Seton scores by putting me through the public colon prep and gets an easy field goal by keeping me from being able to sleep at night; my offense shows up finally by doing the prep while watching the Masters and tacks on a field goal of my own with the interviews.)

On a serious side, we were surprised and a bit disappointed to learn that my concerns about the sacrifice involved in a new heart becoming available and the need to be the best steward possible for any heart that came my way were never expressed to the transplant team doctors by other prospective or actual transplant recipients. Bummer.

ed

From: David Hurta
Sent: Saturday, April 11, 2015 8:53 AM
Subject: Re: DAY THREE

Ed,

You keep playing that "dead man walking" card as often as you like. Nobody deserves a deck full of them more than you. I am thrilled to hear that great things continue to happen on the third day. Jonah emerged from the big fish, Christ arose from the grave, and in a very similar fashion you came back in the third quarter and tied the score with Seton. As you aptly stated a truth so many years ago: "I'm glad we belong to a God who is not a catch-and-release God!"

I recall the words Mordecai said to Esther when he asked her to go in to see the king without her being summoned. "Perhaps this is the moment for which you were created!" When I think of all the combined hours that were spent in schooling, training, and hands-on experience of all the medical and professional staff that have attended to you over the past three days, I am overwhelmed at God's prevenient grace. Perhaps this is the moment for which you were created! Instead of you, what if Sarah, Rebecca, Laura Paige, or Paige was in the hospital? Think how overwhelmed you would be at the resources and the army of medical professionals who were being deployed for the care and restoration of your loved one. Well, this is how all your friends and armor bearers feel about you. So you hang in there and know that you are greatly loved by many and are encompassed by the Peace of God that surpasses all understanding.

I will never leave my wingman!! See you soon.

Bogie 5, over & out

From: Paige Innerarity
Sent: Saturday, April 11, 2015 12:03 AM
Subject: Day Three—the Beat Goes On

My Dear Friends,

So, our story continues in Austin. Friday has been busy with more consultations with the transplant team. We started out with a visit with the team psychologist, who pronounced Ed "not crazy" and healthy "from the neck up." I like Dr. Berg very much. In our family, "crazy" is a somewhat relative term, but I digress. I will save the topic of craziness and eccentricity for another time.

While Ed was preparing for his colonoscopy tomorrow, I slipped away and met my sweet brother, Jim, for a chat and lunch down the street from Seton. I chattered (crazily), Jim listened (dutifully), and I left feeling much better. Jim is wonderful in more ways than I can count. He is brilliant, funny, handsome, calming, and spiritually grounded. He blesses our family just by existing. Caroline and I call him The Golden Child because, as far as my mother was concerned, he could do no wrong. Now that we are all adults, we no longer hold that against him, because it was pretty close to the truth, anyway. We love him as unconditionally as he loves us. (Thank you, Jim, again, for always being there.)

Speaking of Caroline, my sweet sister called this afternoon to tell me she is on her way to Austin tomorrow. Is there anything better than that news? No, there is not. I woke up and learned it was National Siblings Day (which I don't believe is a real thing, except on Facebook) and my brother and sister have made my day! My children, my sister, my brother, my friends—you are my heroes. Never forget how your prayers and your love are lifting us up. Ed and I can never thank you all enough for the support we are receiving from you all every single day.

Life is complicated. Life is hard. Life is crazy. In spite of these truths, I believe Life is beautiful. Every challenge is an opportunity to see God's face and plan in the faces and deeds of friends and strangers. There is so much joy, so much love if we will just be still and open our eyes and hearts. You all have proven this truth to me again and again. Thank you.

Love and Grace,
Paige

From: Ed Innerarity
Sent: Saturday, April 11, 2015 9:12 PM
Subject: DAY FOUR: "Not so far, I taste metal."

To My Armorers whose prayers I feel:

Up early for a colon job that got pushed back until noon. The GI doc talked me into having an EGD (esophagogastroduodenoscopy) to make sure there were not any ulcers or lesions. I was reluctant to have that particular procedure but decided it was best. Every funny thing about a colonoscopy has already been said so I won't try, besides, I got the clean report that I needed to clear a very important hurdle. Plus there are some remaining esophagus and stomach areas that need some attention. I had some stomach issues from the very beginning. Now those can be finally dealt with. The anxiety associated with not being able to breath and thinking I might die has turned my stomach into a little acid factory.

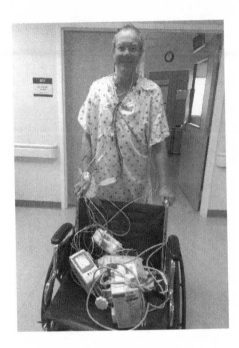

I had been promised I could have anything I wanted for lunch so sweet Paige talked Whole Foods into cutting me a big ¾" T-bone and grilling it to perfection! Life is good.

I got the afternoon off and watched some Masters golf as Paige and Caroline scouted for a nearby apartment. I even had a nap. Looks like I might be here in ICU for a while. I would trade Wolfcamp acreage for a hot shower. Looks like I will be stuck with the acreage.

DAY FOUR SCORE: **Seton 6, Eddie 14!** (Box score: Seton made a touchdown by rule based on the colonoscopy. BUT, the extra point was blocked as the colon blow went too smoothly. Eddie scores touchdowns with the clear report and nap.)

ed

From: Ed Innerarity
Sent: Sunday, April 12, 2015 10:00 PM
Subject: DAY FIVE

"Never cut what you can untie."

—JOSEPH JOUBERT

Today was mostly a day off, which was nice. I did have a handful of doctor interviews, but I was able to take a couple of walks up and down the halls with 40 pounds of wires and pumps and O2 monitors and IV lines so it was hardly like a hike up to Goose Creek.

Although I think of that. I think about the Mennonite tomatoes, that they might taste good again. And the Stirrup and how I miss golf days with the guys and how the hay field is doing without me, and how I miss turkey season with David and Cam, watching Rebecca ride, and hearing from LP about work and hearing how Eleanor is doing and talking sports with Sass. Will I ever get to fly fish for salmon in Alaska again? I wish I could be in my own bed, and how nice it would be to take a shower. I really wish that this was not so hard on Paige, who spends every waking hour trying to think of ways to make me feel better. But for a while, all of that has been set aside, not forgotten, but set aside until I get a new heart. That thought, that goal, is the only way out of this for Eddie. Jordan Spieth was kind enough to provide me a few hours of distraction today with his awesome play at the Masters.

Caroline has been here a couple of days and has been such a big help for Paige, plus a nice distraction from all things transplant. They brought me another big steak tonight with a baked potato and a big salad. Life is good. It really is. At least I am in no pain—none—and not sick at my stomach. I am truly thankful for that.

Another significant procedure tomorrow when they run a device of some sort up and through a vein they cut open in my groin to check on the other side of my heart where they are likely to find an Out of Order sign.

Please pray for sweet Paige.

ed

From: Cathy Manning
Sent: Monday, April 13, 2015 9:36 AM
Subject: Re: DAY FIVE

Ed and Paige—First of all you know I have rallied the troops here in Dallas and my family is praying like all-git-out!!!! Andrew texted that he wanted both of you to know how much he loves and admires you—Ed, he specifically said he appreciated how supportive and encouraging your comforting words have always been to him when he wasn't sure he was doing the "right thing." I'm so glad you have had such a positive influence on him!!! NOW, to the two of you—I cry every time I read the emails—the absolute unconditional LOVE you two have for each other is incredible—you know how very lucky you are to have each other—I hope I find that someday.

Ed, keep eating those steaks, dragging the bells and whistles down the hall, and I'm sure, entertaining all the nurses, doctors, aides, and anyone else that comes your way. You and Paige are truly an inspiration. Life has definitely thrown you guys some curve balls—but with each bump in the road you grow stronger and those of us watching from afar—well, we grow stronger too!!!

I LOVE YOU BOTH WITH ALL MY HEART—there are not two better people in this world!!

XOXO,
Cathy

From: Ed Innerarity
Sent: Tuesday, April 14, 2015 2:48 PM
Subject: DAY SIX

Yesterday started off somewhat inauspiciously. At midnight, I woke up completely covered in sweat—from the bottoms of my feet to the top of my head, my hospital gown, blood pressure cuff, pillow sheets, the whole nine yards. Being the clever guy that I am, I quickly connected the medical dots and realized that I was going through menopause. I had just had my first hot flash, in this case a hot epoch.

The docs all showed up early with what seemed like a setback: The coat hanger in my neck was to be removed. I knew that alone would move me from 1-A to 1-B on the transplant list so I was initially quite disappointed. I later learned that because of the high-powered IV meds, my condition had improved significantly since I was admitted last Thursday and that I would be "sent home" at some point to rest and wait. Yes, that describes me perfectly, rest and wait.

Before I had time to pout, they came and got me for my next heart catheter, this time the left side of the heart. While they confirmed my need for a new heart, the committee that actually lists me would require this test as part of the diagnostic battery. Be careful what you joke about.

You may recall, I said they might find an Out of Order sign on the left heart catheter. They did, and more.

To look at this part of the heart, everyone in the hospital gathers in the area of my groin, and they cut open a vein and an artery so they can insert long soda straws called catheters. These are guided to the heart using magic and celestial navigation and something else using x-rays. Through the catheters, they get a detailed look, along with high-resolution photos of the arteries in the area. My main descending artery was 90 percent blocked. This is the so-called Widow Maker. We are all somewhat confused since I have never had a blockage problem. Mine has been an "electrical" problem, not "plumbing" as they say in the heart business. It is possible that this very new blockage developed because of my ultra-low blood pressure. So, I am hustled back to the room for extra ports to be installed in my left underarm. Then back to the cath lab for the "meet you at my groin, part 2": a balloon and stent treatment for the blocked artery. Time and dehydration did not permit the installation of an additional IV access point, so the balloon and stint job was performed without any sedation. Not how I would have spent my milk money. Everything worked out smoothly, and now I had to only lie flat on my back and not move for six hours in hopes of the groin incision healing enough to pull the soda straws without blood going everywhere. After several hours and a clotting test, the catheters were removed, along with very fresh stitches placed "down there" to close me up. After ice packs, sand bags to curb the bleeding, they finally got it to stop late in the day. Day Six was over.

DAY SIX SCORE: **Seton 31, Ed 14** (The box score would show that Seton controlled the ball and clock most of the day with the offense on the field most of the time. Ed got an early touchdown by the way of his 1-B status. A late touchdown comes from the remedied blocked artery. As they say in this business, any extra blood flow to the heart is a good thing.)

ed

From: Rebecca Innerarity
Sent: Wednesday, April 15, 2015 2:31 AM
Subject: Re: DAY SIX

". . . put your hope in the Lord, for with the Lord is unfailing love and with him is full redemption."

—Psalm 130:7

From: Ed Innerarity
Sent: Wednesday, April 15, 2015 9:25 PM
Subject: GOING HOME TO WAIT

First thought: isn't it interesting that this past weekend a nice young man named Jordan Spieth won the Masters in grand and classy style. His sponsor was none other than Under Armour. That is what I have said you guys have done for me: provided me support, encouragement, and hope in an otherwise difficult time in my life. Sounds like Under Armour to me, in a most spiritual way. You guys are my spiritual sponsors.

This morning at 7:00 a.m., I was approved by the Seton Heart Transplant Institute to be placed on the list for a new heart. I could get a call for the heart at any time starting right now. It could also take weeks or months, we simply do not know. I am being placed as a 1-B, meaning immediately available. The only class above me is 1-A and that is for people with at least one medical device and at least 2 IV meds keeping them going. The 1-A patients are confined to the ICU. Right now there is one guy in my same area that is 1-A and he is looking for a much smaller heart than I could take.

In my favor, I am blood type A positive; I passed the pulmonary test, antigen test, current cardiac status, right and left catheter exams, TB tests, various hepatitis and pneumonia vaccinations, 40 blood tests, liver profile, kidney tests, chest x-rays, a colonoscopy, along with an esophagus and upper GI inspection.

It is now 9:30 p.m., so let me wrap this up. I am now on the list for a transplant. I am sorry there was not a minute to reply to you because we were covered up with doctors every minute until late this p.m.

Life is still good, however much of it is left.

ed

From: Caroline Cowden
Sent: Thursday, April 16, 2015 7:57 AM
Subject: Re: GOING HOME TO WAIT

Ed, you forgot the cytomegalovirus test which you also passed making your options for a donor much greater!!!! I can't thank you enough for letting me be there with you and Paige to witness this indescribable experience! Watching miracles happen every day was something I will never forget! You have been an incredible witness to all you have come into contact with at Seton and many outside of the hospital that have never met you but heard your story from Paige! Your will, courage, humor, and most of all, faith will continue to get you through this journey! I love you, dear Ed, and you will continue to be in my prayers!!! You are at THE TOP OF THAT LIST!!!! God has you and Paige in the palm of HIS hand and HE has great plans for you! I pray for peace as you now sit back and wait, which I know is SO hard!!!

TWO OF THREE DAVIDS
(BY PAIGE)

I do not care for math. There are still times I wake up in a cold sweat because my nightmare is that I am staring at a semester exam in algebra or geometry (I never even considered taking calculus) and every single proof or equation is completely beyond me. Without divine intervention or blatant cheating, I am doomed. I am feeling more than slightly queasy just writing this.

I love numbers, however. I use the patterns and sequencing of numbers every time I design a piece of jewelry. The significance of numbers comes up time and again in history, nature, literature, superstition, religion, geography, medicine, architecture, engineering, cooking, and culture. That is the short list. Numbers are everywhere and in everything.

Let's take the number three: The Trinity, Three Graces, Three Coins in a Fountain, Three Strikes, Three Chances, Three Wishes, Three Stooges, Three Tenors, Three Musketeers, Three Branches of Government, Three Peas in a Pod, Good Things Come in Threes, Bad Things Come in Threes, Three Blind Mice, and the list goes on and on and on.

My list of "threes" includes Three Davids: David Koch, David Hurta, and David Terreson. Two of the Davids have been around, well, almost forever.

David Koch came into our life by marrying one of our best friends, Barbara Tompson. Ed and Barbara's friendship goes back to the cradle, literally. Their mothers were great friends and were in Midland Memorial Hospital the same week for Ed's and Barbara's births. David has been a friend for over forty years and our shared memories, triumphs, and tragedies with him and Barbara are too many to count. We have gone through the Starving Graduate Students phase together, which included shared suppers in each other's apartments, bowling, racquet ball and tennis competitions at Trinity, camping, rafting and fishing trips, and endless card and board games. The entertainment was cheap or free, but the fellowship and conversation was priceless. Later, we had three girls and so did they. When both couples ended up raising our families in Midland, we ended up neighbors. To this day, through various house changes, we still live within walking distance of each other. This was not by plan or design on any of our parts, but I do not believe in coincidences. So, when the chips were down, what did David do? David did everything.

When Ed went into his free fall of congestive heart failure, he became incredibly withdrawn and began to shut down physically, emotionally, and spiritually. I begged him to tell his friends, and his reply was, "Tell them what? Tell them I can't walk five steps without gasping for breath? Tell them I lie in bed hurting all over? Tell them I am dying? They don't need to hear that. I don't need to bring down my friends." But one Sunday afternoon, as he was laboriously walking the neighborhood with me, trying to "get exercise and feel normal," we dropped in at the Kochs' house. We sat on the sofa, and he told them everything.

He told them he was in afib, that he was seeing David Terreson in a couple of weeks to hopefully get his heart back into rhythm. He couldn't get his breath, he had no energy, he felt terrible. Of course, David Koch had already noticed he was not well. When one is in congestive heart failure, trying to "act normal" looks like that—acting, but very poorly. Our friends listened. They asked questions. They were empathetic and engaged. The circle of people who knew widened, and our burden was shared. It was a cathartic time of grace for us, with many more to follow.

David Koch did not just ask, "What can I do?" David did things. David walks Willie Nelson, their family Shih Tzu, every night. When he walked by our house, he would pick up Babe, our yellow Lab, and take her with them. He did this the whole time we were in Austin, for weeks on end. He and David Hurta would fight over who was going to take care of Babe, feed her, play with her, and check on the house. If he saw a sprinkler head that was malfunctioning, he changed it. He called Ed about once a week just to tell him about that week's golf game, talk about football or Jordan Spieth, tell an off-color joke—just two guys talking. If Ed wanted to talk about his week of labs, pre-hab/rehab, or doctor consults, David listened and asked questions. They talked about everything and they talked about nothing. Because Ed did not have the physical stamina or the emotional collateral to engage with all the people he knew were praying for him and cheering him on, having David as the conduit to his circle of friends, keeping him vicariously involved in his regular life, was important.

Did I mention David is a clinical psychologist? His children, when they were younger, said David was not a Real Doctor. Perhaps, before any of us were even born, God knew we would need an Unreal Doctor for a lifelong friend.

Which brings me to David #2. David Hurta has been Ed's wingman (David's description, not mine) for over thirty years. They have played golf and shot dove, pheasant, and quail. We have all snow skied together and taken our children to Disney World. These guys have caught catfish in the Rio Grande along the Texas-Mexico border in their younger days at great peril and fly fished for trout on the Rio Grande near its headwaters in Colorado. They have eaten more meals together in Styrofoam containers, driving down the highway to another adventure, than they have shared at an actual table.

After Ed and I were in our apartment in Austin for a few weeks, it became apparent a trip home was necessary. Ed was in a routine, with daily workouts at the hospital, so he decided that I could leave him to take care of things at our house, and David Hurta could come be his babysitter for a couple of days. I was not thrilled about leaving Ed. His milrinone infusion pump/batteries had to be changed every seventy-two hours, as well as the IV bag of milrinone. The medication forced his heart to beat more efficiently. The bag change had to be done by (me) wearing surgical gloves, carefully cleaning all the connections to the pump and PICC line with alcohol, turning the pump off, turning it back on, checking the digital readout, flushing the line if it was not working properly, and knowing when it was working properly. I had been trained at the hospital for this task, and the thought of turning it over to anyone else made me extremely nervous. Thankfully, Ed was also scheduled for a dressing change, which was done by a home nursing service. The visiting nurse could also change out the pump and IV bag, so David could just be the babysitter and have no medical responsibilities. It was a great relief to me.

Ed has always been incredibly self-reliant. One crippling aspect of a critical illness is a loss of independence. The last thing I wanted, and the last thing Ed needed, was for him to feel suffocated by me being overly protective and ever present. We had spent virtually every moment together now for months. A break from one another would be good for both of us. I agreed to go to Midland as long as he promised that he and David would call if there were any issues or questions. David flew in to Austin as I drove home to check on the house and dog and to bring back things we wanted. The pump and bag change were scheduled for the next day.

David was an attentive observer but was just that, an observer. The visiting nurse did all the actual procedure. After all, with a trained professional, what could possibly go wrong? The boys left the apartment, giddy with success, and went to have a putting contest at Hamilton Golf Course, right down the street. Ed could not understand why he felt so weak walking up the small slope on the putting green. He figured that it was just heat and humidity. Ed won the contest, but they went back to the apartment because Ed was feeling *really* crummy and needed to lie down. After a bit, and feeling steadily worse, Ed called David into the bedroom and said, "Something is wrong. We might need to go to the hospital. Let's check the pump."

The nurse had not turned on the infusion pump after completing the dressing, pump, and bag changes. Now, Ed should have checked it himself instead of assuming that all was in order. He made a quick call to Rick Aristeguieta at Cardiac Infusion Specialists, who talked them through a saline flush; the pump was started and all was well. Of course, David was horrified and shaky. He had actually had to "scrub up and glove up" to do the saline flush. Rick is an awesome coach and talked him through it in his quiet, confident manner over speakerphone. Ed's reaction? "Hurta, you should be upset. You just got beaten in a putting contest by a guy who was mostly dead. That must be a bummer."

When Ed recounted the story to me over the phone that evening, I was initially weak in the knees. Why did I go to Midland? In what universe did I think Thing One and Thing Two could have managed an infusion bag change? What if Ed had ended up in ICU because I went to pick up a few clothes for us and pat Babe on the head? Auugh! At this point of imagining the worst, the end result required my focus.

Ed did not end up in ICU. Ed and David, with Rick's calm instructions, fixed the problem. The crisis was averted. Ed felt empowered and a little less sickly and dependent because he figured it out without me there yammering in his ear. We had a respite from each other, and time with one of his favorite guys in the world made him feel, however briefly, normal. It was a definite win for Team Innerarity. Yes, it all turned out just fine.

I never left him overnight again.

PART 2

The Waiting

*"It was about waiting for your dreams and not knowing
if they will come true. I always felt it was an optimistic song."*

—TOM PETTY

We left Seton Hospital, spent one more night at the hotel, and then moved into a furnished apartment a couple of blocks and a straight shot from the hospital. Going to Central Market for groceries was, literally, a walk in the park. We walked through a park with our grocery bags to shop, sat outside and ate lunch or supper, and heard live music on the weekends. Ed bought a bike to ride to the hospital for his sessions with physical therapy, but he rode the bus back to the apartment because even riding up a slight incline was impossible. His decision to ride the bike to therapy was met with disapproval by some of the staff, citing the traffic dangers, the possibility of falling, getting overheated. "Really?" Ed said to me, "I am a dying man! I am not going to worry about traffic risks at this point! I've got to have some normalcy in my life!"

Achieving any sense of normalcy was elusive as we waited. Meals were strange. Ed ordered multiple items, ate a bite or two, and said everything tasted like copper pennies. He choked down his meal supplements and continued to lose weight. I shopped, I cooked. I threw away food and felt terribly guilty for the wastefulness of it all. We waited.

Waiting in an apartment can be incredibly boring and nerve-racking. Field trips around Austin were imperative to retain sanity and to keep us from the fate of "The Gingham Dog and the Calico Cat." (Read the poem if this reference does not ring any bells.) The Bob Bullock Texas State History Museum was a field trip. We went to Mayfield Park several times to see the peacocks, strolled around a bit, and sat and watched the families corralling children. I wondered if Ed would live long enough and be strong enough to be able to take our granddaughter on outings. At Christmas, he had been too weak to pick her up and could only hold her sitting on the sofa. We waited.

The LBJ Museum had a retrospective exhibit of The Beatles. We loved reliving our shared memories of how they changed music forever. Ed can't carry a tune in a bucket, but he has a tremendous appreciation and knowledge of many different artists, particularly from the '60s, '70s, and '80s. Our three daughters grew up listening to The Beatles, The Beach Boys, Bob Dylan, John Denver, Joan Baez, Joni Mitchell, Linda Ronstadt, Lyle Lovett, songs from Broadway musicals, Gilbert and Sullivan, and more. These were our soundtracks for car trips their entire childhoods. Would we ever crank up the music at the cabin and sing along with these songs again? I wondered. And we waited.

Thank God it was the summer of Jordan Spieth! This young man from Dallas had played golf briefly at the University of Texas and was lighting up the PGA with his brilliant playing. When Jordan was playing a tournament— which was, fortunately, most of May, June, and July—Ed and I watched every drive, chip, and beautiful putt on television. Under Armour sponsored Jordan Spieth. I studied the shirts he wore, went to Academy Sports one morning, and came home with three of them for Ed. He was enchanted! He wore a Spieth shirt every time we watched Jordan play. I wondered if Ed would ever play golf with his buddies in Midland again. He was a 4 handicap at the time he got so sick in November. And we waited.

We talked. We talked about our family, friends, and medical team. We exchanged observations and thoughts about what we had each heard in meetings with doctors, nurses, physical therapists, pharmacists. It was always good to have two viewpoints, two sets of ears. Everyone listens differently; everyone has different impressions and filters conversations in a highly individual manner. It was a good thing to rehash those conversations and compare notes. Sometimes we argued; sometimes we became frustrated, but we laughed a lot, too. We waited.

We wrote. We poured out our thanks, our hopes, our gratitude in emails. It was therapy for us; it helped us remember that we were fortunate in so many respects. We lived in an age and a country where great strides were being made in medicine. In our lifetime, the first heart transplant was performed. In our lifetime, organ donation and transplants were becoming more and more commonplace and successful. How incredible and humbling to be part of this life-saving story. It was scary, it was exhausting, but it was a great adventure, and even in the midst of it, we were very aware that this experience was a privilege. We waited.

We discussed the donor and his family. We spoke of the donor as "he" because Ed's size and body type pretty much excluded the possibility of his donor being a female. Ed wrestled with the fact that someone else's life would end in order for his life to continue. He agonized over that loss. He spoke of, and still speaks of, someone losing a father, a son, a brother, a spouse, and it is a grief that he will always carry. With that grief is an intense gratitude and desire to be the very best steward of his new heart. Ed may never meet the donor family, but he and I will pray for them every night for as long as we live. The decision of the donor and his family to donate Life is a gift we are always aware of and will appreciate forever. We prayed for the unknown donor and his family, and we waited.

From: Ed Innerarity
Sent: Thursday, April 16, 2015 7:41 AM
To: My golf group
Subject: Ed out for golf for a while

Guys,

Most of you have probably heard part of this by now but I wanted you all to hear it from me. Just before Easter I met with a new doctor in Austin at the Seton Heart Institute. After an exam, I was told that my heart was weaker than previously suspected and they wanted me back ASAP. We spent a wonderful Easter with the entire family (Sarah and Cameron, LP and baby Eleanor, and of course Rebecca) doing all the fun country things, turkey hunting, exploring the woods, having great family meals together, etc. I also had the chance to tell them about my upcoming plans to enter the potential transplant program at Seton.

I returned to Austin right after Easter and beginning last Wednesday I began a weeklong and very detailed diagnostic program. In the process I was tested for every possible illness, vaccinated for even more, and my heart tested and worked on. I was also blood typed and my antigens tested for a potential heart match. The purpose of the weeklong stay was to evaluate me for a possible heart transplant and get me in as good of shape as my heart might permit. I had multiple catheter treatments, one of which discovered a major blockage in the Widow Maker. That blockage was remedied as part of the process. I also had a new colonoscopy, upper GI inspection, multiple chest x-rays, pulmonary tests, and the list goes on and on.

The bottom line is that yesterday the Seton Heart Institute Transplant Committee placed me on the list for immediate transplant. That does not mean I get a new heart immediately, but that I am immediately available to receive one if a suitable match is found. The transplant listing is very complex, but I am seeking a certain size heart from a donor with a certain blood type and with certain antigen matches. Some people get a new heart in just a few days, others have not gotten one after more than a year. I am behind some previously listed potential recipients, but ahead of many.

Anyone overweight, or a smoker, or with lung, kidney, or liver issues is essentially listed after me. I am very blessed that I met all of the criteria and in the eyes of the committee, present a nearly ideal host body for age 63.

Paige and I have gotten an apartment here in Austin for the wait. We are likely here until I get a heart. We could use your prayers, of course, for the perfect heart, for Paige, and that the heart go into the best possible host, maybe that is me, maybe that best match is someone else. While we need your prayers, we also need time to rest and prepare. Except for family, we are not seeing visitors. The time to ourselves will be needed to prepare for the biggest battle of my life, the transplant operation.

So I am out for golf this weekend, but let's hope I will be back on the course with you guys sometime.

ed

From: Ed Innerarity
Sent: Thursday, April 16, 2015 8:38 AM
To: John Delatour
Subject: Summertime plans

John,

After a weeklong cardiac evaluation at Seton Heart Institute here in Austin, I was placed on the heart transplant list. I will not trouble you with the details of the past week, but I went through every test I had ever heard of and then some. After the weeklong process, the heart committee listed me as "immediately available." This does not mean I will get a new heart immediately, just that I am available if a suitable match became available. In theory, I could get a call tomorrow or six months from now that my match had been found.

I had a surprising good spot on the list because of my size, blood type, antigen make-up, and "host profile." In other words, I have no other health issues. I am writing this to you guys in hopes that you might pass along the word to all of the Wason families. [These are twelve families, including ours, who jointly own a ranch just outside Creede, Colorado, on the Rio Grande. Each family has a summer home there on the river. This is some of the best fly fishing in the state.] Paige and I have gotten an apartment in Austin a block from the hospital where I continue to be tuned up as an outpatient and made as ready as possible for the transplant.

[It is noteworthy that I had just seen John and his golf buddies at lunch a couple of weeks prior at a tiny general store in Garner, Texas, just a couple of miles from our farm in Parker County. I was with our cowboy and probably looked as if I had been on the tractor all morning, which I had been. Little did I know at that time what major changes were in store for me. I hope I did not look like someone who needed a new heart, but you will have to ask John and his buddies about that.]

Please pray for the perfect heart and that it go into the host body that will be the best possible steward, maybe that is me, maybe that is another recipient, but that is our hope. While we need your prayers, we are also seeking some time alone to recover from the past week and to rest and ready ourselves for the biggest battle of my life. I will be consumed with pre-surgical preparations and rehab, but please feel free to email Paige.

With God's grace, we will be back to Wason one day soon.

ed

From: John Delatour
Sent: Thursday, April 16, 2015
Subject: Re: Summertime plans

Oh Ed, what earth-shattering news. I can't imagine yours and Paige's stress. We will pray for you and I will share your story with my friends who are all Christians. You looked great by the way. Stay well, my friend, and let us know if we can help in any way.

John and Ann

From: Ed Innerarity
Sent: Thursday, April 16, 2015
Subject: Re: Summertime plans

John, we consider ourselves very blessed and very fortunate. Many would not have made it through the evaluation phase nor received a listing for a new heart. I am also quite blessed to otherwise be in good shape. We decided to view this as a celebration that an opportunity exists for me to return to Wason and golf and everything else I love and miss. The actual transplant will be difficult, I am sure, but I am ready. Thanks for your words of encouragement and your prayers.

From: Paige Innerarity
Sent: Thursday, April 16, 2015 9:03 AM
Subject: A Favor, Please

Dear Friends and Potential Gate Keepers,

I have picked you all to make a very special request for a huge favor. The news we received yesterday has humbled, thrilled, and overwhelmed us. After months of watching Ed decline dramatically, and a week of grueling tests, interviews, and medical procedures, he has received what may be the equivalent of The Golden Ticket. Most of yesterday was spent with Lisa, the nurse coordinator of the transplant team, briefing us on what lies ahead. It is daunting, to say the least. Bottom line, Ed needs rest. He needs time to get himself in the very best shape possible for the transplant and aftermath. We have no idea if and when the phone call will come that his heart has been found. We have no idea how he will do during the surgery and post-surgery. Transplant recipients are receiving a great gift. Along with this gift come great responsibilities and a whole new set of challenges—psychologically and physically. What we need from you all is that you communicate to everyone else how much we need to have this time to rest, reflect, and Just Be.

Right now, by necessity, our days and nights are filled with preparation for the days ahead. Please tell our friends we love them, we appreciate their love and concern, we covet their prayers, and know they are storming the gates of heaven on our behalf. When they ask what we need, the answer is very simple. We need to be alone. We need to have them show their love by respecting our need to settle in to what will be our new life going forward. Besides our children and family, we simply cannot and will not be able to have visitors for a while. I say this firmly and unapologetically because Ed's well-being has to be my only concern right now.

Thank you for understanding. Thank you for loving us. Thank you for all of this and more. Feel free to email or call me any time. I want to talk, I want to write. If I don't answer, you understand.

So, I am going to consider this a spiritual and physical retreat for Ed. I will write an email to that effect sometime, maybe today.

Love and Grace,
Paige

From: Ed Innerarity
Sent: Saturday, April 18, 2015 9:53 AM
Subject: OUR NEW AND NORMAL LIFE

Note to self: Stop expecting any good, or as they say in bow hunting for fish, aim low.

Friends,

Paige and I have moved into a very nice apartment she found that is only a couple of blocks from the transplant hospital, and we are rapidly making this our new life. Our new normal life. After the past four months in general and the past week in particular, this looks and feels like normal to us. We are in the same apartment complex that our oldest daughter, Sarah, lived in when she was at UT in the late 1990s. So, maybe it's a little weird at our age to move into an apartment (which just happens to be where our daughter once lived while in college) but besides that, our new life is normal.

Ok, it is also a little weird that I have to wear a shoulder bag with a pump inside with a bag of juice that is continuously pumped through a thin tube through a semi-permanent port under my left arm directly into my aortic valve. Replacement bags of Heart Alive juice arrive by FedEx packed in commercial grade freezer bags every 72 hours, but besides that, our life is normal. I forgot to mention that I sleep, eat, and shower with my little bag of juice and pump attached. Every activity is accompanied by this companion. I have found a way to hang the bag on a coat hanger twisted to attach to the top of the open linen cabinet so the tube that carries the juice makes its way to me in the shower, coming in from the left side, of course. But besides that, life is normal. Oh, and the bags of juice have to be refrigerated until 90 minutes before being placed in service, and when a new bag is hooked up to the battery pow-ered pump, a second and identical pump is always used so that at any given time both pumps are available in case one malfunctions. What is not normal about that? And, we have 10 days of backup batteries on hand and eight days of backup juice in the fridge and multiple sets of backup tubes and connections and dressing connections. Plus a sack full of sterile set-up kits with gloves and masks and drapes to replace any part of the tubing or dressing in case of a break or tear. A nurse comes by every few days to make the sterile IV changes, but Paige is checked out on pump changes, battery failures, or if the line needs to be flushed with saline solution before, during, or after a blood draw. Other than that, our life here is normal.

Normal and almost boring; that's us. I look like a well-groomed drug user, what with the needle marks in both arms, the back of my hands, my neck and groin, so except for that, I guess normal would describe me. Although, I am not exactly sure how I would describe my now famous groin area where I had multiple catheters, one in a vein and one in an artery. The same area where a collection of ICU nurses collec-tively worked somewhat unsuccessfully to stop the bleeding. (Somehow it seems that I should have gotten money for that, or flowers.) The same area that looks like I took a Nolan Ryan fastball and where I now have a hematoma the size of Johnny Bench's catcher's mitt. But, besides all that, our lives are pretty much normal.

Very normal. Unless wondering what each cell phone call might bring. Or, being unable to sit on the patio of many a nice Austin restaurant and not wonder who else shares my blood type. Or, wanting to tell the young father dining with his wife and little girl next to us to please don't get killed by a drunk driver. Or, wondering how in the world I am to be a worthy host for a heart that becomes available only because someone's Dad or brother or son lost his life. Or, how desperately I hope the transplant team makes sure that if a match is found for me, that there is not someone else on the list that might not need it more or provide a better host body. Or, how my soul is touched just sitting in the same waiting room with others that are in the transplant program, knowing that nearly half of the group will go on to Glory before a match is found. I would like to think that these thoughts are in fact normal, at least for someone on the transplant list.

ed

Coreg: A drug that works by blocking the action of certain natural substances in your body, such as epinephrine. This effect lowers the heart rate, blood pressure, and strain on the heart. Coreg belongs to a class of drugs known as beta blockers.

From: Ed Innerarity
Sent: Saturday, April 18, 2015
To: David Terreson
Subject: "Fly" Fishing

David,

Even though I am stuck here in Austin in our little apartment while waiting for the call that a matching heart has been found, I wanted you to know that I am still able to do some fly fishing. Perhaps not the same fly fishing that we enjoyed together in Colorado, but under the circumstances, it may be the only fly fishing I might be doing for a while.

Behind our apartment here just a few blocks from Seton is a walking park with a couple of ponds, with the usual ducks, turtles, small fish, and kids running around. Add to that the drone that my children gave me for Christmas last year. It has been in the box since Christmas because I had to get a second pacemaker the next week. I had a friend bring us some things from Midland last week, including the drone. I tied a few feet of fishing line to the drone, attached a small hook on which I placed a small quantity of premium Boar's Head Ovengold Roasted Turkey Breast from Central Market. I dangled the line in the water, carefully avoiding the turtles, which would have pulled the drone under. I made a beautiful presentation, just beside some rocks where the fish were likely to be. On my very first drift I hooked up with a native Travis County Pond Perch. I must admit that the walk down to the water's edge would be a bit too much effort in my current condition, so I had one of the numerous little boys that had gathered around safely return the fish to the water. In the remaining 10 minutes of battery life left (for the drone, not my pacemaker), I caught two more, all about the same size. I am attaching a picture as fishermen seem required to do. If there is not a picture, does that mean they made up the story?

I know you are proud beyond belief and probably jealous that I was able to do some fly fishing while on the transplant list and attached up to my infusion kit. And you are stuck in the office listening to other bad hearts.

Your friend,

ed

From: David Terreson
Sent: Sunday, April 19, 2015
Subject: Re: "Fly" Fishing

Ed,

That is a remarkable achievement. You are an extraordinarily creative guy.

There is but one issue. As a fly fisherman, you understand that catching a fish with bait, no matter if you are a little infirm, is not fly fishing. I feel bad about being a little harsh like this, but I'm sure you will understand.

David

To: David Terreson
Sent: Wednesday, April 22, 2015
Subject: Real "Fly" Fishing

David,

Not exactly sure who made you the Cardio Commissioner of Fly Fishing but your point is well made. I made Paige drive me out to Bee Cave to the fly shop and I bought an assortment of flies: prince nymphs, hoppers, and a Parachute Adams. Then the trudge back to the pond with drone in hand.

While I would have preferred to use a dry fly, the prop wash from the drone ruined the effect so I quickly tied on the bead-head nymph. It worked just like when you and I fished the back channel at the Stirrup last year. First drift, too. I think it was the same little boy that released the fish for me. Maybe the same fish, but either way I can check the pond on 38th Street off my bucket list of places I always wanted to go fly fishing.

Requisite picture attached. Let's hope I make it through all this and we can do some real fly fishing again someday.

ed

From: Paige Innerarity
Sent: Monday, April 27, 2015 9:43 PM
Subject: There's Nothing Like a Farm

One of our favorite movies of all time is *The Natural*, starring Robert Redford as Roy Hobbs, an over-the-hill baseball player with a past who comes back to the game. If you haven't seen it, you really must. I will not get into the story, but toward the end of the movie, Roy says, "There's nothing like a farm," and proceeds to expound on the subject for a while.

Really, you need to see this movie.

This past weekend, Ed received a much-needed break from medical appointments, consultations and phone calls, and we drove to the farm, near Weatherford. Rebecca lives there and runs Little Feather Equestrian Center, her hunter/jumper operation. She has a tiny house and an amazing business that is growing like Topsy, and she loves it. When we visit, we live in an old double-wide that is referred to as the Bunkhouse. Rebecca thinks that sounds better than "old double-wide." It is really perfectly adequate. The carpet in it is new, it has four window unit air conditioners, a stove that works reasonably well (as Cameron Ferguson can attest after preparing a scrumptious standing rib roast Easter weekend), and well water that has a distinctive sulphur smell but still gets the dirt off after a day working and playing outside. Eleanor Innerarity, our 14-month-old granddaughter, believes the Bunkhouse beats the Broadmoor in every respect. There is nothing in there that she can destroy, nothing in there that can hurt her. She can run around in the Bunkhouse until the cows come home and no one will tell her no. It is heaven for a toddler.

The farm is beautiful. It has been a labor of love for Ed for the past two years. He has built beautiful fences and horse paddocks by welding oilfield pipe that covers a couple of miles. He has designed and supervised the building of a beautiful tank that he stocked with fish last weekend now that the farm has been blessed with abundant rain. He has met with the county agent and learned how to grow hay. Through those efforts, the farm is self-sufficient in feeding all of Rebecca's horses on the coastal Bermuda we grow or trade for alfalfa. He has learned how to operate a HUGE tractor and spends hours doing farm chores with it.

Seeing the hay growing in beautifully, the creek running big, the tanks full of water for the first time in two years was the best medicine in the world. We drove around the hay field in the mule, marveled at the lushness of the grass Ed planted last year around Rebecca's arena, watched Rebecca work horses, laughed when I dumped minnows (accidentally, of course) in the bed of the mule and had to race to get them in the tank, enjoyed the steaks Rebecca cooked for our supper together Friday night, and dreamed of the future.

Making plans, thinking of the future, watching the light in our daughter's eyes as she spoke of new friends, wonderful neighbors, and her growing opportunities with Little Feather Equestrian Center and Tiger Lily Farms made for a pretty nice time. [Tiger Lily Farms is the name of our farm and Little Feather Equestrian Center is Rebecca's horse training and lessons business located on the property.]

By the time we drove home Sunday, Ed and I were exhausted. We talked all the way home about the fun we had. We were so grateful to have a 48-hour pass to play outside and see the changes since Easter and all the rain we have been blessed to receive. Again, we looked to the future and to plans Ed has for more improvements, more projects. Is it any wonder that I agree with Roy Hobbs?

There's nothing like a farm.

Love and Grace,
Paige

From: Joe Gifford
Sent: Thursday, April 30, 2015 11:42 AM
Subject: Thinking of you

Ed—We were really shocked to get news of your heart problem yesterday. You are certainly deep in Emily's and my prayers. But knowing you, especially from your great tennis playing days, you will rise up and win the match.

I have had heart experience there in Austin at St. David's hospital. A Dr. [Jason] Zagrodzky did an ablation to heal my rather serious atrial fibrillation. That was several years ago, and I am good as new now—and you will be too. I talked to Zach Graham (landman at Devon yesterday) and he said there were no immediate plans to drill on our block, but they were pleased with the way some of the wells were holding up. They are still drilling in other areas nearby.

I'll be at your side to help you win this match.

Best regards,
Joe

"I don't need other people, I don't need help,
I can take care of myself."

—JIMMY STEWART (AS JEFF WEBSTER IN *THE FAR COUNTRY*)

From: Ed Innerarity
Sent: Sunday, May 3, 2015 10:45 PM
Subject: Are we there yet?

On long trips, I am the guy that scribbles how many miles I drove in the past hour, each hour of the drive, so I have a running total of average MPH during the trip. I am the guy that can start the gas pump in Roswell at the Circle K and dash to the men's room and back just as the gas pump clicks off. Not a wasted minute. Back when I played golf and back when I went to Colorado, I would often make the drive after playing 18 holes with the guys on a summer Saturday morning. I made sure I was in the first of our two groups, and I would order a hamburger and fries to be ready and waiting when I walked off the 18th hole, ready to jump in the car and head north. No wasted time.

To me, driving time in the car on longer trips was really time to catch up on calls, think about deals and generally do something productive. Maybe just do something, anything. No reason to waste any time. I have the restaurants between Midland and Creede on speed dial so that my dinner at Gabriel's north of Santa Fe will be ready when I drive up. Ditto for Bar-B-Q places between Midland and Weatherford. No points earned for waiting. Call ahead seating: go for it, no reason to wait. Need 15 gallons of paint for the farm; call and have them mix and shake it and have it ready. No stars for having to wait. Need to get the tires rotated and balanced; call ahead and reserve a time and have lunch while they are working. Need to service the car at the dealership; email for a time so there is no waiting.

And there is nothing wrong with calling Tractor Supply to see if they have the Red Lion water pumps so that they might hold one at customer service. Save some time, less waiting. Ditto Home Depot for

14-inch cut-off blades; ditto Vogel's orchards to see if they have peaches. They don't give corner offices to people who spend their lives waiting.

I am the guy that schedules my dentist and dermatologist appointments for first thing after lunch to avoid waiting. And there is nothing wrong with calling ahead of time to make sure "we are running on time." You don't get bonus points in life for just waiting in line.

But I am waiting now. Waiting for the call that they have a new heart. Waiting and waiting. My cell phone is always with me. My speed dial numbers and most frequent contact numbers are the heart clinic and transplant nurse. I am waiting for a heart. Not the same as waiting for tortilla soup or industrial paint but waiting nevertheless.

Unfortunately, waiting for the call entails much more. I am connected to a plastic tube that runs from a small pump and bag with half a liter of important heart juice into another plastic tube that goes into a vein on the inside of my left arm to my heart. I eat, sleep, work out, shower, drive, pack the car, unpack the car, cook, clean, shave, get a snack out of the fridge, walk across the room, or walk into a restaurant with my bag of juice and pump. It doesn't matter that I put the bag inside a small backpack so I don't look so much like a "dead man walking." Pride. Sometimes pride is capitalized, sometimes it's underlined. Either way, I am waiting for the day that I don't have to have this bag over my shoulder.

ed

From: Mark Petry
Sent: Wednesday, May 6, 2015 6:55 PM
Subject: Fishing some day?

Ed,

I was thinking of the Mother's Day caddis hatch earlier this week when my daughter, Kelby, shared with me that you have recently been diagnosed with a serious health matter. I was sorry to hear this news and what you must go through for a full recovery. I only wish the best for you and your family. Please know that my thoughts and prayers are with you. Let me know if there is anything I can do to help. Take care.

Regards,
Mark R. Petry

From: Mark Leaverton
Sent: Monday, May 11, 2015 6:48 AM
Subject: Checking on You

Ed, I cannot tell you how many times the Lord has put you on my heart. This morning at five when He awoke me was one of those times. Vicki and I continue to pray for you and trust God's perfect timing for you. It was more than a blessing to talk to you in mid-April, just hours after you were put on "the list." I trust that you are not climbing the walls too much on 38th Street! When you get a moment, drop me an email so I can know how you are doing.

Give our love to Paige (we are praying for her too).
Mark K. Leaverton

From: Paige Innerarity
Sent: Tuesday, May 12, 2015 8:30 PM
Subject: NO NEWS IS . . .

Time passes and I realize that not only are the natives getting restless in Austin (insert Paige and Ed for "natives"), but also the rest of our tribe—our friends and family. I have emails and texts asking if we have any news. Well, I wish we did, but we don't, and the fact is, we won't.

There is really no news in the heart transplant biz until the phone rings, we are informed that it looks like a match, and it is time to dash to the hospital. It gives me chills to even think about The Call. It is my last thought before I fall asleep and my first thought when I wake. The Call is on the edge of my thoughts all day, every day. It is my hope, my prayer, my deepest desire at any given time. In between my thoughts about The Call, we have our present life in Austin. We walk, we talk, Ed goes to cardiac rehab, I go on more walks. We shop, I cook, we laugh, we fuss, and we make up. We talk to our children, we write, and we read. We live and plan and dream about the future. So, I guess that, in this case, no news is no news.

I have to believe that all this waiting around is bringing us ever closer to The Call. I have to believe that this is time that is necessary for Ed to prepare, mentally, emotionally, and physically, to be the best recipient of this precious gift. Believe me, we get discouraged! The entire transplant team told us that waiting for a heart is incredibly stressful and nerve-racking. They were right. It is dreadful. My mama always said, "Hope springs eternal in the human heart." I am clinging to hope, hanging on by a prayer, and thanking God for the saints, here and in heaven, who are holding Ed and me together.

So, once again, thanks for being there. Thank you for loving us. Thank you for hanging in there when you get no news. We will send you news when we have something to report.

Love and Grace,
Paige

From: Ed Innerarity
Sent: Wednesday, June 10, 2015 10:22 PM
Subject: Day 66—Cardio Rehab

People suffering from Stockholm syndrome come to identify with and even care for their captors in a desperate, usually unconscious act of self-preservation.

Friends,

I feel compelled to set the record straight. I may have mentioned that I was headed to "cardio rehab" or that I had just finished my "cardio rehab." That is what they call it and that is what the sign on the door says. It is even what Blue Cross complains about on my EOB (Explanation of Benefits), but it should be called something else; for now I will refer to it as cardio *pre-hab*. It is equal parts Vacation Bible School, Gold's Gym at 5:45 p.m. on a weekday, ICU at a nice metropolitan hospital, and the exercise yard at Shawshank Prison.

The ratio of instructor to instructed is about the same as VBS, something over 1 to 1. It resembles Gold's Gym because of the huge assortment of treadmills, NuStep recumbent elliptical trainers, weight lifting stations, and various colored elastic bands and hand weights. The similarity to an intensive care unit comes from the sheer number of stethoscope-draped, scrubs-wearing, blood pressure-taking nurses with large three-ring binders with way-too-much medical information about their charges. Plus, the assortment of brightly colored and neatly labeled crash carts, oxygen tanks, and preponderance of emergency defibrillators is a nice touch. I assume you have all seen *The Shawshank Redemption* and the various scenes in the exercise yard. Despite their varied backgrounds, crimes, ages, and ethnicities, the inmates form a bond and develop a feeling of "us against them."

Now you have a mental picture of the cardio pre-hab facility. It is located right next door to the "something wrong with my heart" clinic and the transplant office. So my day goes something like this: Wake up and get reminded immediately that I am tethered to a 22 oz. pump and 510 ml of "special heart juice" and 33¼ inches of very important tubing that transports the SHJ from the bag, through the pump along the 33.25 inches of tubing into a PICC line inserted under my left arm. The PICC line was fed into an important and otherwise unsuspecting vein that travels through my shoulder, under my collarbone and on to my soon-to-be pawned heart. Along the way, the PICC line shares the vein with one of the leads from my new pacemaker to ol' shaky. [I looked up what PICC stands for, but I passed out partway through. I know that P stands for *pain*, the I for *intense*, and one of the Cs for *can't believe I let them do that to me.* Maybe one of the docs on this email list can help out with the whole name. As I said, I passed out reading about it.] The PICC line is also used for blood draws every so often except when we are unable to get a blood return. This is often cause by a clotted line. When that happens, they do certain things that also contain the letters P and I.

So after I make breakfast and take a shower (never straying more than 33.25 inches from my friend) I get dressed and wheel my new bike outside for the short ride to the hospital. For nine minutes I am free and pretend nothing is wrong with me, my pump and bag of juice tucked unobtrusively into a cool Osprey day pack, and no one who would see me knows. FYI, I do wear a bike helmet, because I do not want to take any unnecessary risks before they cut me in half and plop a new heart in there and wire me shut.

Before you know it, I am at pre-hab, which I must admit, is probably the highlight of my day. The staff there is not so happy about the bike ride. As soon as I walk in, one of the many nurses/physical therapists weighs me, takes my blood pressure, and hooks me up to a heart monitor. We all start off with the treadmill; it is part of the plan. Part of our rehabilitation/punishment is Kelly Ripa. She and Michael Strahan are always on the flat-screen TV right there in front of the treadmills. Has anyone else ever wanted to slap Kelly Ripa? Is she really perfect? At everything? Did you know 50 Cent's real name is Curtis Jackson? But not to worry, that's over at 10 a.m. so we get to watch *The View* with Whoopi Goldberg. And now Raven-Symoné is permanently one of the hosts. [Apparently, she wasn't so permanent after all, as she's no longer on *The View*.] Be still, my erratically beating heart.

At first they took my blood pressure at every workout station. Now, they just come by and show me a chart with "self-perceived effort levels" and ask how I feel. In the exercise yard, you learn quickly to say "about an 11, Boss" or "I'm at level 12, Boss." If you report working harder than that, you are told to go get a cup of cold water and go sit by the blood sugar testing station. (I am not making this up.) If you report working below level 5, the incline is raised, the speed is increased, and you receive a mild electric shock. (OK, maybe I made that up about the shock, and we don't refer to them as "Boss.")

The goal of the hard-working staff in Room 512 is to prepare me for "major surgery." The better shape I am in before the transplant, the better my chances. There are frequently 8 to 10 of us working out. Many have diabetes; many are trying to lose enough weight to make the transplant list; many recently had a heart attack or had a pacemaker installed or a stent inserted. A few are there with new hearts. Some can barely do any exercise, others quite a bit. I am the lucky one out of the group. I am in no pain. My pacemaker is doing a great job along with my special heart juice. My size and history of being active and trying to stay in shape will be a big help come transplant time. Plus, I am ready.

I come back from pre-hab pretty much spent. I try and catch the 10:23 a.m. or 11:08 a.m. Cap Metro bus to take me and my bike up the hill to the apartment. Only a couple of blocks, but after pre-hab a bit more than my old worn-out heart can handle. If I missed the bus, I would slowly trudge up the hill walking my bike like the pitiful person I must have looked like. If I did catch the bus, they would have to wait for me to load my bike onto the front of the bus. First the front tire, then the back tire. Who could possibly lift all 18 pounds of a bicycle at once? After the second week, the driver would not let me pay my 75 cents, since I was only going 600 yards.

But I look forward to the next day like I am getting ready for something. I remember how difficult the first several weeks after my knee replacement were. I got through that thinking of what Baron had gone through with his knee the year before. [Baron Batch and his brother, Brian, are considered members of our family, though not formally so, as in adoption. Their mother died when Brian was a senior in high school. Some families in Midland opened up their homes for the boys to live in, and we were one. Baron was a standout running back in college at Texas Tech University and later played for the Pittsburgh Steelers. He got his knee torn up his first year there and had to have it rebuilt. A year later I had my knee replaced.] Now, I think about all that I have lost because of my heart problems: this summer in Colorado with the family, fly fishing (anywhere) with any number of friends, golf with my guys, not being a prisoner to this apartment, not being tied to this tubing and bag, working at the farm, and more. The pre-hab is perhaps the only daily way I have to prepare. I am doing what I can to prepare for this battle. No guarantees, but with each workout, I tell myself I am slowly tipping the scale in my favor. I can't make the phone ring with a call that a match has been found, but if it does, I need to have done all I can to prepare and give that heart a fit body to live in.

I guess we are all preparing for something.

Live well, like today is the day.

ed

> PICC line: A peripherally inserted central catheter is a form of intravenous (IV) access that can be used for a prolonged period of time (e.g., for long chemotherapy regimens, extended antibiotic therapy, or total parenteral nutrition) or for the administration of substances that should not be done peripherally. It is a catheter that enters the body through the skin at a peripheral site, extends to the superior vena cava (a central venous trunk) and stays in place (dwells within the veins) for days or weeks.

From: David Hurta
Sent: Wednesday, June 10, 2015 10:55 PM
Subject: Re: Cardio Rehab

I am the luckiest guy in the world to be one of your many wingmen. You are to this heart transplant mission as Doolittle was to the Tokyo raid—prepared, ready for battle, and stacking the odds in your favor for victory. Sleep well and have another great day at pre-hab in the morning! Bogie five flying cover.

From: Monica Gose
Sent: Thursday, June 11, 2015 11:49 AM
Subject: Re: Cardio Rehab

Every time I think I feel crummy, I just think how I would readily take this pain if it would magically make a heart appear for you. You are my hero. You are an amazing man. Keep it up!

Love,
Monica

From: Ed Innerarity
Sent: Wednesday, July 1, 2015 6:14 PM
Subject: DAY NINETY-THREE

"Do or do not. There is no try."
—YODA, *THE EMPIRE STRIKES BACK*

I was dead asleep when Paige sat on the edge of the bed and said that "Lisa just called and they may have a heart." Lisa is my primary transplant nurse and everything goes through her. (If I leave the county, when I get back, changes in meds, problems with meds, dressing changes, PICC line issues, questions for the doctor, appointment with the doctor, weight loss issues . . .) Everything. We had been in Midland just a couple of days earlier and yesterday was my first day back at rehab after a few days off. I was still tired from trying to play golf over the weekend, and I had done a little extra at rehab Tuesday morning so I was worn out and still hard asleep at 6:30 a.m. when the news came. Paige cried for a bit, then said a prayer, then resumed crying (happy tears, as she would say).

Running out of options, my primary cardiologist and my electrophysiologist (both good friends) referred me to a new CHF (congestive heart failure) expert, Dr. Cishek. I met with Dr. C on March 31 of this year and was told I was very sick and that without a transplant, I would not make it to Christmas. It was a new heart or hospice. That was 93 days ago, but that is in geologic terms, or so they always say to make things seem to be very distant in time.

I had rehearsed this day so many times that with each trial run, it was as if the real date was being pushed further and further away. I had also prepared myself for a subsequent call saying that a problem had been found or a matching test did not go well, but with each call from Lisa, the likelihood of a match seemed to increase. "Looks like noon." "When did I last take my meds, when did I last eat, how are we doing?" "Get ready, but stay there." "Probably more like after lunch." "What does Ed like for breakfast? Polenta. OK, he can have that." "Tests going well so far." "No issues with the heart so far." "Maybe the middle of the afternoon." "Relax but don't do anything or get away from your phone." "Other organs being allocated first."

Funny where you get inspiration. Maybe it's not inspiration, but for me, it's like a really tough climb. It is curious where you sometimes find a solid foothold to help with the climb. Jordan Spieth starts every match assuming he is already two holes down. In his mind, he has to find a way to win two holes just to get back to even. He has prepared himself to work extra hard. He has prepared himself to win. Works for me.

The calls are coming every 30-45 minutes, not to me, but to Paige. I thought I might run over to rehab and burn off some nervous energy. Nope. I was thinking about riding my bike to the transplant hospital to gather my thoughts. Nope. All that was left was to fly my drone. I took it as high as it would go and with the GoPro was able to shoot a video where I could see the hospital over the top of the apartments and downtown Austin in the distance. Beautiful partly cloudy day.

I was told I could have something clear to drink and one clear liquid to eat before 1 p.m. so we drove over to Hoover's and got an Arnold Palmer without the Arnold. Just lemonade. By the way, how is it that a clear liquid is considered something to eat? Anyway, I swing by the rehab center to tell the ladies "I won't be coming for a while" and to tell them thanks for all the help. It turns out that having to watch Kelly Ripa all those mornings did not kill me, but rather must have somehow made me stronger.

More calls. The heart has now passed all the screenings including CDC. I finally speak with Lisa and learn that several hearts have been offered (to my team for possible use in me) and that those were declined (for me) for various reasons; size was cited as one reason, none of the other reasons were disclosed. It doesn't really matter. I ask Lisa two questions, "Is she happy with the heart being offered?" And as much as I really want and need the heart, are they sure that one of the others in my transplant group might not need it just to make it through the week?

The donor situation has bothered me from the start, that a life is lost for the heart I am about to get in the next few hours. That donor and his family will be going through the worst of times and at the same moment, my life is changing in a positive way because of his selfless act. Ninety-three days into this and that is still something I think about every waking hour.

The other question is also tough for me. Without any doubt, and with 99.9 percent certainty, all of the others in my transplant group that

I have met at the clinic or at rehab or at one of the support group meetings, all of them struggle significantly more, hurt more, and seem more engaged in a hand-to-hand battle with just staying alive than I. I pray that the doctors make the right decision because I could not.

More calls and now it looks like a go. "Make sure you are all packed and ready, but just sit tight." "Probably later this afternoon or evening." No problem, I like starting off two down. As promised, Paige and I call the girls when it first looks like a go, to do so prematurely would be unfair given the chance that something might come up. Reading between the lines, it almost sounds like the donor is local or certainly close by. We are never told that, but the fact we are being asked to stand down at the apartment makes me wonder.

Finally get the call saying to show up at ICU at 3 p.m. Glad I shaved my chest this morning. After we parked the car, we got a selfie of us at the ER helipad. Like getting ready for the big game. Checked in, lab work done, sticky things on my chest, fresh chest x-ray, reams of paper-work, hospital gown, and it is just now five in the afternoon. Surgery has been moved back again this time to 8:30 p.m. Working on finding a home for all the other organs.

Not sure how much longer I can type the narrative before they take my laptop and start. It is 6 p.m., and they are about to get sharp things ready for me in a cold room.

Thanks to all of you for your help in so many ways. See you in a few days.

Live well, you don't know about tomorrow.

ed

[*Song #2*. Attached to this email was a link to "Slip Slidin' Away" by Paul Simon, a repeat of the song linked in the DAY TWO email of April 9.]

From: David Koch
Sent Wednesday, July 1, 2015 6:45 PM
Subject: Re: DAY NINETY-THREE

Ed. COURAGE.

David

From Jim Kemper
Sent: Thursday, July 2, 2015
Subject: NOT FINISHED YET

I'm not a very good runner. I don't even enjoy it much, but I run about 2–3 times per week, just to get a little exercise and relieve stress after a long day. I don't run far or fast because I can't. I just run a couple of miles, get a sweat going... and get my heart rate up. That's what got me think-ing a few weeks ago, while I was running around my neighborhood.

It was a few days after I'd visited Ed in the hospital, as he was undergoing his transplant candidacy workup.

As I slogged along over the asphalt, I became keenly aware of my heart, thumping in my chest, and I thought of Ed. I thought of how many times I've run and taken for granted the blessing it is to generate an accelerated heart rate. I thought of how Ed can't do that right now.

Then, I thought of the labor his heart endures for each precious beat, and I felt even more thankful for a blessing I've just expected, almost to a point of ignorance. I realized every beat is a gift. During ONE year, at an average of 80 beats/minute, our heart beats 42,048,000 times. Over Ed's 63 years, his ticker has fired off around 2,649,024,000 times (give or take a few 10,000). Honestly, how does ANYBODY'S heart do that? Why?

Because God decides the exact number of beats to allow before He stops our pulse.

Throughout this odyssey, we all wonder, "How much longer can Ed's heart beat?"

God will decide when He is finished using Ed here on earth. It's clear He's not finished yet. He's not finished with Ed, and He's not finished with Ed's heart. So, He keeps it beating. He keeps it beating, with a doctor like David or with a pacemaker or with a drug or whatever the vanity of this world claims as the "reason" Ed's still upright and breathing, but ultimately, HE is the one who decides when He's finished with Ed's heart and when He's finished with Ed.

. . . He's not finished yet. There are more people to add to the countless, fortunate individuals whom Ed has impacted and blessed.

It's 1:00 a.m., Ed went under anesthesia at 12:05 a.m., as he visited and joked with the anesthesiologist. His heart is still beating, for a few more hours . . . God's not finished yet.

Somewhere, within a few miles, lies a lifeless man whose chest contains a beating heart. His family is grieving. His life here is finished. God finished molding him here on earth and will, very shortly, perfect him in paradise.

But God's not yet finished with his heart.

And as soon as God flips the "off" button on Ed's heart, that tired, motionless sac will be removed. Through the gift of science and skilled surgeons, God's going to place that generous soul's heart into Ed's chest.

And, miraculously, that heart will resume its job, pumping along, almost as if to exclaim in a thumping clip, "not/yet, not/yet, not/yet..."

He's not finished yet.

Jim Kemper

From: Winsome McIntosh
Sent: Thursday, July 2, 2015 at 5:45:02 AM
Subject: Not finished yet

Paige,

What strength you both have. I know you are tired of "being strong," as I am, but frankly part of God's plan is to test our strength, too. Part 1 of Ed's story is done. The agonizing wait is over. For both of you. Your donor lives on, Ed lives on, and you live on. With the hard work of recovery and support ahead, time for you, Paige, to get as much rest as you can. Take a sleeping pill if you have to. Your strength is Ed's strength in these coming days. Know my heart and mind are constantly with you both. If you need me, I'm there in a heartbeat, so they say. And there are many more of those ahead for the Innerarity family. Thank God.

Winsome

"Friendship, generous and unforced, without duty or obligation—
that was surely the foundation of all love that mattered."

—ANNE PERRY, *BLOOD ON THE WATER*

HARVEY
(BY ED)

Harvey is the valet parking czar at Seton Hospital. They might be full, but Harvey can always find or make room for one more vehicle. After all, the passenger is almost certainly about to have some procedure, and a smooth valet experience is often the first Seton impression. And usually a good one.

Harvey's gentle demeanor belies the obvious fact that he probably played linebacker somewhere important and hurt people on the football field. I met him about the time I went on the transplant waiting list. We had moved from Midland and gotten an apartment just a few blocks from the hospital and clinic next door. At first Paige would drop me off at the hospital for my nearly daily check-ups, lab work, rehab sessions, or emails. At night, I would email my medical updates to my family, but without Internet at the apartment, I would sneak onto the Seton Wi-Fi to send them. Harvey would let us drop rein the Toyota for long enough to borrow some bandwidth.

Later, I would buy a bike and helmet and ride the few blocks for my Seton runs, so I got to see Harvey almost every morning. "Hello, Mr. Ed." "Looking good this morning, Mr. Ed."

"Any news today, Mr. Ed?"

There is a kolache shop between our apartment and the hospital. I quickly learned that Harvey liked the fruit-filled ones just as much as the sausage-filled, so I usually got one of each and let him pick. Things changed after the transplant. No more bike, too much strain on my recently severed sternum, so it was back to Paige taking me to the hospital, this time for my weekly biopsies.

In one of these little stories, I include a description of the *right heart catheterization with biopsy*. Not my favorite, not for a long time. I was told specifically not to drink anything after midnight. I was also told by my doctor not to come in dehydrated, so I drank plenty of water as soon as I woke up until I checked in at 6:15 a.m. I was so scared of the biopsy; I walked the few blocks to the hospital to drink more water and to prepare myself for the pending doom. Attitude is everything. Besides, the walk got my blood moving and would make it easier for the hurt team as they inserted various things into otherwise innocent and harmless veins. Paige took the car and was already inside by the time I had finished off one last bottle of water and strolled up to the valet parking in the predawn darkness.

And there was Harvey. I am pretty sure he got the surgery schedule from the doctors, and on days I was scheduled to get the business, he was there waiting. I know he was nervous and scared just like me, but he always pretended to be calm and matter of fact. "Morning, Mr. Ed." "When are we going fishing, Mr. Ed?" He was trying to trick me into not being so scared, but I was not fooled. I was probably going to die. Probably from the IV alone.

Most of the time I survived the biopsies; in fact, I think all of them so far. And Harvey was often there when I was wheeled out to help me into the car. He was smiling. Always smiling. I think he was smiling because I would be back soon for another biopsy.

I hope I get to go fishing with Harvey someday.

PART 3

Heart of Gold

*"I found the task so truly arduous . . . that I was almost tempted to think . . .
that this movement of the heart was only to be comprehended by God.
For I could neither rightly perceive at first when the systolic and
when the diastolic took place by reason of the rapidity of the movement."*

—WILLIAM HARVEY

When Dr. Hunter Kirkland walked into the waiting room in the wee hours of the morning on July 2, he had a big grin on his face.

(Ed and I had met Dr. Kirkland at 11:30 p.m., when he popped in to introduce himself right before Ed was wheeled into the OR. He asked if we had any questions. I replied, "Yes, Dr. Kirkland, I have just one: Have you had a nap?" Dr. Kirkland squeezed my hand, smiled, and said, "I just woke up. I am well rested." This confirms what I always suspected: Transplant surgeons are like astronauts and naval aviators—they can fall asleep instantly to prepare for what lies ahead.)

My brother, Jim; David Koch and Grant Billingsley (two of Ed's loyal golf buddies and close friends); and I all stood up to greet Dr. Kirkland. I hugged him and asked him one question: "So, Dr. Kirkland, how many shocks did it take to get Ed's new heart to wake up and start beating?"

"None," he replied. "I took off the clamps and it started right up."

How is that possible? I relate more to William Harvey's words from four hundred years ago than I do to what Dr. Kirkland said. Medicine has changed and advanced exponentially in my lifetime. Who knows what the future holds? As I stood in that waiting room—euphoric, grateful, giddy, and exhausted—I realized that our lives had just changed completely, again. The waiting was over; a donor heart was beating in my husband's chest, and, complications notwithstanding, the hourglass had not run out but had been flipped over. Finally, Ed had received his Heart of Gold.

For the next twenty-four to thirty-six hours, Ed was on a breathing tube and heavily sedated. When he was awake—well, sort of awake—he was agitated. Ed's biggest fear pre-surgery was of having a stroke. Every time he was conscious, he wanted reassurance that he had not had a stroke, that he was going to be fine, and that the new heart was working. Since he couldn't speak because of the breathing tube, he thought he had lost his speech. Since he was on heavy doses of drugs, he had no memory of our telling him he had not had a stroke and the heart was perfect. It was Groundhog Day every time he woke up.

Eventually, the breathing tube came out, the heavy-duty drugs cleared his system, and his brain fog abated. Our children hugged and kissed him goodbye and returned to their respective homes. Ed's beloved physical therapists from cardio rehab came several times a day and supervised longer and longer strolls down the hall. In no time, Ed and I were allowed to go outside on the fifth-floor patio—Ed pushing a myriad of monitors and machines in a wheelchair. It was July in Austin, and the temperature was approximately 220 degrees, but we would find a patch of shade, survey the beautiful Austin skyline, hold hands, talk, laugh, and think about the future.

I realized that for the past six months, we had only thought of the future in the short term—dinner plans, a field trip, what medical appointments Ed would have that day or the next. Suddenly, Ed's life stretched out and opened up like a telescope. Through the eyepiece, he could see himself in the future, his health and life restored due to a complete stranger. Yes, we talked about that donor. We wept for him, for his family and friends who were grieving their loss while our family and friends rejoiced at Ed's new life. Their lives were being reset too.

One week post-transplant, we left the hospital and moved back to our little apartment for a few weeks as Ed settled into the routine of biopsies, cardio rehab, and the ever-changing medications and protocols that needed to be followed to keep his new heart healthy. By August, we were able to go to our cabin in Colorado for a whole week. It was incredible to be there. We took walks, Ed fished, and we drank in the tranquility and spiritual peace that the river and mountains always granted us. The three trips to Creede in August and September were a major turning point in resetting our life. This place felt normal; this place gave us back ourselves.

By the end of September, we had turned in the keys to the Austin apartment and moved back to Midland. Our trips to Austin would continue, but they were less frequent with each passing week. Ed, who had lived his life so abundantly before his transplant, had been entrusted with a new heart and given a new life. The experience has marked him and changed him in ways that are still being revealed, but the realization that this entire experience, with all its ups and downs, is in itself a gift and an adventure has brought about one of the biggest changes that I have observed. Knowing that he has received more time on this side of heaven makes every day precious.

Immunosuppressive drugs or anti-rejection medications inhibit activity of the immune system to prevent the rejection of transplanted organs and tissues such as the heart, kidney, liver, or bone marrow.

From: Ed Innerarity
Sent: Tuesday, July 7, 2015 5:15 PM
Subject: Alive again, I think

[This email was not previously sent. It was a very difficult email for me to write at the time, not only physically but also from an emotional stand-point. I was able to get my thoughts down—being plagued with hiccups the first couple of days didn't help any, among plenty of other things, as you'll read—but I just wasn't ready to share what I was experiencing with my family and friends at that point.]

I think the early astronauts had an expression for going around the dark side of the moon. They were out of communication for a while and lit-erally cut off from the rest of world. I am back from being on the dark side of the moon.

The actual transplant surgery began very early on July 2nd, and I was kept sedated until earlier today.

Until my head cleared I did not know if I had had a stroke . . . I could not swallow. Rebecca gave me ice chips when the breathing tube came out.

Josh, one of the guys from rehab, came by to help me stand for the first time. I remember saying, "Do I look like I want to put my feet on the floor/to stand and take a step?"

I was given so much anti-rejection medicine in the past two days, my eyeballs literally changed in shape. As a result, my vision was so bad I could not write and my hands were shaking so much I could hardly use the keys on my laptop. And where is Lisa? And shouldn't someone make sure that my chest isn't going to pop open and whatever they put in there fall out?

It is a strange place where they turn you off and hand you over to the heart/lung machine. Stranger still that twilight where you are aware enough of what's going on that you're sure something is wrong but too sedated to see the dots, much less begin to connect them.

They brought me scrambled eggs and I remember looking at them for many minutes hoping I might remember how to use a fork to transfer hospital eggs from the divided sectioned plate to the middle of my face. Aim small, miss small, my ass.

My sternum itself did not hurt, or if it did, everything else was demanding my attention so I did not notice. Everything they had done made something hurt and all the anti-rejection meds made me feel sad.

The one overarching thing that got me through today was knowing, or more accurately, being told again and again, that it was over. The surgery was over. The transplant was over.

"The trouble is, you think you have time."

—JACK KORNFIELD, *BUDDHA'S LITTLE INSTRUCTION BOOK*

From: Ed Innerarity
Sent: Wednesday, July 8, 2015 9:52 AM
Subject: NEW DAY FIVE: "Home team bats last."

Day Five.

As you may have guessed, I am starting over on the day count beginning with the procedure. If you get a new heart, you get to do that. Days start over, time resets, life continues but renews. Yes, it has been about a hundred days since I first saw Dr. C, but I have a new watch and a new calendar. And except for biopsies and clinic visits, the new calendar is mostly open, waiting for important things I need to do to be written in it.

I am still 63 years old, but the days from here on will somehow be counted differently. They like to say "in geologic" terms. Like dog years or horse years or heart years, these will be different in some way. In time, I will learn how those days are to be lived. In his email, Jim (Kemper) has made me aware that I have more work to do and that Someone must still have plans for me. I am beginning to learn of those plans. Plans for me, but why me?

The last few days have been something of a blur. I do recall that one big prayer was answered in that as they prepared me in the final minutes before the surgery, I was not scared. Completely peaceful. I was acutely aware that I might die, but not scared. I was as prepared as I was going to get from the reflection and from the rehab. Nothing worse than going into a big battle being scared, nothing better than an unexplained calm. I was being stuck with everything you can imagine, and it was as if I was watching them from across the room, still there but unaware of the sticks and lines and drips and preps. Nothing the anesthesiologist or surgeon told me gave me any fear. That is one big answer to one big prayer.

Curiously, just the last few days before the surgery, I told Paige that something was changing, that things were not quite right. Looking back, it is likely that the heart juice was slowly losing its effectiveness on my heart. Maybe the same for my rehab, that I had maxed out the benefits from the exercise. My side effects were slowly becoming more pronounced. I was beginning to develop new side effects to the meds, the heart failure, and the treatments. My new pacemaker was now assisting with each beat in a desperate race to see if it could keep me going just long enough for a new heart to show up. That pacemaker lasted only six months and was taken out when the new heart went in, but played a big role in keeping me going and strong until the big day. Same for the heart juice. I was developing a skin reaction to the meds, too. I was running out of time.

I will not bore you with the surgery details; I slept through most of it anyway. I was vented for about 36 hours afterward. Then, they started pulling things out. First, the breathing vent, which felt like a piece of corrugated culvert pipe. Then various catheters in various places. Then chest tubes and arterial lines and wires and such. I remember trying to write important questions on a clipboard: Did I get my new heart, did I have a stroke, do I have a heart mate? Why me?

Paige and everyone else assured me over and over, but I was too drugged to really understand.

Live well,

ed

[*Song #3*. Attached to this email was a link to "Why Me, Lord?" by Kris Kristofferson, which pretty much sums up how I felt. Laura Paige headed back to Denver earlier that day and bumped into Kris at the airport. When she called to tell me, I immediately thought of this song.]

From: Stuart Beal
Sent: Wednesday, July 8, 2015 10:01 AM
Subject: Re: NEW DAY FIVE

Thanks for the update, Fast Eddy! Thinking about and praying for you daily. Headed to Wyoming with dad on Saturday to try to catch a 28+" rainbow. Will be thinking of you as the river flows between my feet. Pictures to follow.

From: Mickey Trimble
Sent: Wednesday, July 8, 2015 11:25 AM
Subject: Re: NEW DAY FIVE

So glad to hear from you. I am happy things are going so well and know that you are on the road to an amazing recovery. Love the song, but you know WHY as well as anyone. God still has things for you to do in this life, as Jim so eloquently put it; He isn't finished with you yet.

Blessings and comfort as you continue on this road of recovery,
Mickey

"I feel a very unusual sensation—if it is not indigestion, I think it must be gratitude."

—BENJAMIN DISRAELI

From: Ed Innerarity
Sent: Thursday, July 9, 2015 9:48 PM
Subject: NEW DAY SEVEN

Time to start saying thank you.

Paige does Facebook, and each day she reads me the encouraging words from so many people. Many I hardly know or only met recently. But apparently, all those prayers and all that support and all that encouragement worked because I am doing very well. I am on a ton of important medications, and I am not out of the woods yet, but they pulled out the last of the chest drain tubes and external pacing wires today. (The pacing wires are like small sewing needles on the end of thin wires strategically driven into the chest and abdomen in case the new heart needs pacing or shocking. But it has not needed that.)

To each of you (and many others I don't have email addresses for), I want to say thank you. Because each of you were there when I should have been afraid, but was not; when I should have really hurt from the surgery, but did not; when I simply could not have taken any more sticks, IVs, PICC lines, stitches, but did; when there was every reason I could die, but did not. It is exactly as if you were there instead of me for the worst of it. Taking what I could not, hurting so I would not, getting cut open so I did not have to, being wired shut so I could be spared that, too. Every hurtful, painful, scary, or anxious event of this ordeal (including knowing that on any day I could very well die or have a stroke) was shared by each of you, all of you, time after time. And usually, when I needed help the most. Somehow just saying thanks doesn't seem to quite cover the tab.

I have had some time to reflect and have come to the conclusion that in our lives we all have lists. Mine includes a list of people to thank, and that list will always (should always) be the longest list. There is always someone out there that deserves a thank you from me. Wish I had said thanks again to my eighth-grade science teacher, my freshman economics prof, Dr. Wyvell, a special guy that taught me how to string a tennis racket, that guy that introduced me to rocks, Paige's aunt . . . Trust me, it's a long list and the names on it may not mean the same to you. But the names on your "thank you due" list will. We become who we are in large part because of those folks.

The other observation is that we all have a list of regrets, but this one is hopefully much shorter. The shorter the list of regrets, the better. Ditto for the list of people we need to apologize to. I do not think these two lists are the same. I have few regrets in my life. I would give anything to have gone to one more football game with my dad, nothing to apologize for, but something I regret we did not do more of.

The need to tell someone I am sorry about something I did gets a little tricky. Unlike regrets, I can make that "sorry" list as short as I want. For me, my regrets are missed opportunities. Many missed opportunities are gone forever, and there is nothing I can do about them now. Maybe they become life lessons we can learn from.

But maybe every unspoken "I am sorry" is a regret where the cement has not yet hardened. I still have time to do something about it. My new heart has given me the chance to work on shortening my "I am sorry" list. Please be patient.

Again, thanks to all of you who helped walk me through this. Any of you who know me at all agree that this is not me, this medical stuff is not my deal, and that there is no way Eddie could do this. No way. So that leaves you. You made this possible. You will want to say it was the Lord working through you, of course. But you asked for and accepted the assignment. Accepting the pain, sharing the hurt, shouldering the fear, refusing to let me die. I may be wearing my donor's heart, but I am wearing a smile that came from all of you. I can't help but think of the song "Heart of Gold" by Neil Young.

[*Song #4.* Attached to this email was a link to "Heart of Gold" by Neil Young.]

—╢╱╲╱╲╟—

From: Paige Innerarity
Sent: Thursday, July 9, 2015 11:22 PM
Subject: A THANK YOU NOTE

On December 3, 1967, Dr. Christiaan Barnard, a South African cardiothoracic surgeon, performed the first successful human-to-human heart transplant. There were 30 people in the operating room, including Dr. Barnard's brother, who assisted him. The surgery lasted a bit over nine hours. The heart recipient lived 19 days. I remember how electrifying this groundbreaking surgery was at the time, the possibilities it opened for those with heart disease. It received worldwide attention, the medical equivalent of a NASA space launch. I was 14 years old. Ed was 15 years old. He didn't know I existed, and I had fallen in love with him when I was in fifth grade and he was in sixth grade, but that is a story for another time.

On July 2, 2015, at approximately 2:00 a.m., I sat in the ICU waiting room with my brother, Jim. Amanda, the OR nurse, called me with a surgical update: Ed's new heart had arrived and was about to be put in his chest. There were 12–14 people in the operating room, the surgery had begun at 12:05 a.m., and Amanda would call me again about 4:15 to tell me that it was finished. As I write this, I get goose bumps all over again. How can this even be done? What makes it possible to take a heart, which is not beating, and sew it in, take off the clamps, and it is "Gentlemen, start your engines"?

Medicine has come a very long way in a very short time. Technology and surgical skill are to be applauded, and God knows, our family is forever indebted to the doctors, nurses, and technicians who have shepherded us through this process for the last 10 years. God also knows that as a 14-year-old watching Chet Huntley and David Brinkley on NBC News, I couldn't fathom that Dr. Barnard's breakthrough would lead to my husband's life being saved almost 48 years later.

The really stunning epiphany I had during my transplant slumber party that night has nothing to do with science and medicine, though. The amazing, marvelous, miraculous part of the story for me was that during the slumber party, while the person who has shared my life for over 40 years was lying on a steel table, his chest open and empty, kept alive by a bypass machine and the skill of some amazing men and women, we were being propped up by the prayers and hopes of people all over the world. Friends and family were loving us and interceding on Ed's behalf for healing and restoration. An ICU transplant nurse joined us at the slumber party before the surgery was over. David and Grant, two of Ed's golfing buddies and partners-in-crime, drove all night from Midland to join our vigil before the surgery was over. I felt completely at peace and surrounded by the comfort of the Holy Spirit.

I don't know how our story will end. I don't know if Ed will have complications with infection, stroke, or rejection. We have no guarantees in this life, except that none of us will get out of here alive. What I do know is that we are loved, and we can never express our gratitude for that love sufficiently.

So, I thank you all, and I thank my God, the Creator of All, for giving me and my family the opportunity to have some more time with my husband, their brother, their uncle, their father, and their grandfather.

Love and Grace,
Paige

⎯⌁⌁⎯

From: Ed Innerarity
Sent: Saturday, July 11, 2015 8:40 PM
Subject: NEW DAY NINE

Dear Team,

I was discharged late yesterday and we staggered to the apartment and collapsed. Paige was completely spent—me too. It was nice to sleep on our own sheets and without someone trying to draw blood at 3:45 a.m. and then come back to weigh me at 4:15 a.m.

I have had a chance to run the first set of numbers and thought all of you might want to know the extent of the burden you just shouldered.

All of you share in this amazing "taking one for Eddie," but I have it in my mind that each of you had different roles at various times.

Beginning October 31, 2014, I went into atrial fibrillation so you guys have been on the job going on nine months. The afib was masked by acid reflux and an enlarged liver complicating the diagnosis until I was shocked back into normal sinus rhythm on December 10th. First big ouch for my intervener(s). Very ragged December then an emergency pacemaker/defibrillator on January 2nd. Ouch, ouch! A few days later they tapped and drained my lung (thoracentesis). Ouch, ouch, ouch! You guys are pushing and shoving for a place in line to lift me up. I don't realize it yet, but a small army of angel warriors is out there knowing what I don't know. Things would get worse, much worse, as I am being prepared. By now I am unable to walk across the room in the evening. Nearly hourly episodes of acute shortness of breath. I am gasping for air and my exercises to deal with that are not working. My band of warriors was readying themselves for a condition I was refusing to admit that I had, advanced congestive heart failure.

By this time, my dear and devoted cardiologist and electrophysiologist are throwing everything they have at the problem and are unable to even slow the decline. By now I am on some serious meds, but no help. I am taking more diuretics than all the Real Housewives of Beverly Hills. Still no help, but no problem for my band of angels, standing in for my defense with swords in hand at the door of my hospital room. My heart numbers are appallingly low across the board. How I function at all is a mystery to the doctors; they say my body is compensating. I say otherwise.

Out of sheer love and desperation, my heart doctor for the last 10 years, and with a breaking heart of his own, turns me over to a congestive heart failure/end of life/transplant specialist at Seton Hospital. I am told that I will not see another Christmas without a heart mate (an external heart pump) or transplant. I am told that hospice is my only other option. My transplant cardiologist is a petite, no nonsense red-head, and her frank assessment takes away what little breath I have. I am admitted to the Seton Transplant Evaluation program where I end up in ICU for a week. Things are starting to get really tough on my teammates as the team takes a constant series of body blows on my behalf. I have 48 hours to "get my affairs in order." Hats off to everyone who made that happen. Let me assure you, I am not the guy that likes to get a new will, power of attorney, advanced medical directives, and specific orders to the medical facility "just in case." When the lawyers hand-deliver a big pile of important documents, where they say critical things four different ways on 100 percent cotton bond paper, with multiple witnesses and notaries all bound in those blue document covers, you know you are in some serious soup. That is just earthly stuff, but the load on Paige just increased exponentially.

Within a few days, I was placed on the transplant and heart pump listing. [*By coincidence,* just before all this happened, Mickey (my long time office manager and much more) updated and renewed our group insurance plan. We were pushed into a plan I had doubts about, but it would turn out to be exactly what we needed. As I said, *by coincidence.*]

A brief aside: On day three of my ICU stay for the evaluation, I go into a very serious irregular heart rhythm one night as I am asleep. A cardiologist and pulmonologist and crash cart team are standing outside my room eyes focused on the heart monitor at the nurse's station. Can he work himself out of this "spot of bother"? Will he arrest? How long can we let him struggle before we must begin the most dire of situations: proceed with the artificial pump? Paige and I were told exactly what is involved and we were all but required to consider that option to be on the transplant list. We signed the release, but Paige was instructed to intervene before that began. I would wait for a new heart. Period. No heart pump, too risky, too invasive, too many possible complications. Even if it meant that things would end right there. My new pacemaker had been built with a very sophisticated algorithm built in to try to defeat potentially fatal irregular heart rhythms. But that algorithm is not activated for the few months after implant so that the new device can "learn" the nuances of my heart and customize its pacing function.

Fortunately and miraculously, the irregular heartbeats subsided, the crash cart was moved back to the nurses' station, and the on-call cardiologists made their notes in my files. No LVAD for me tonight. Thank you, team, for that.

93 days of waiting, 93 days of agony for sweet Paige and my family. But also 93 days to prepare physically at rehab and mentally here in Austin. My family is tested as never before, but each of them leads a full battalion of angel warriors in full battle gear. They simply will not give up or let me go until a new heart is found. It was during these 93 days of preparation that Paige and I realized that I had already won. Paige actually spoke those words.

All told:

- 40 days of afib
- 1 set of paddles for the heart shocking
- 3 transesophageal inspections
- 19 chest x-rays
- Nearly 40 peripheral blood draws (12 of which are unsuccessful)
- 3 PICC line insertions (one unsuccessful, one had to be de-clotted)
- 5 groin or jugular catheters
- 44 blood sugar finger sticks
- 1 surgery to insert a new pacemaker
- 2 procedures to pull out pacemakers
- 32 infusion pump changes

- 32 bag changes of milrinone (all done by Paige)
- 93 days of milrinone infusion
- 93 days of wearing the infusion kit
- 156 saline solution injection flushes
- 1 emergency flush on a clogged PICC line
  (done by David Hurta no less)
- 1 colonoscopy
- Nearly a dozen immunizations/vaccinations
- 2 thoracentesis procedures
- 3 chest tubes
- 1 large catheter (purpose not to be disclosed)
- 8 temporary pacing leads
- 1 high-performance, high-speed, reversible,
  fine-tooth bone and gristle power saw
- 26 external sutures
- Several internal wire cardiac sutures
- 1 stent for the Widow Maker
- 2 Swans
- Oh, and 1 new heart

You guys have been busy.

Let there be no mistake, this is not "a woe is me" note; this is a "blessed am I" note. If anything, woe is you guys for all the time on your knees, for the sleepless nights, the churning stomachs, worried sick for me, scared for me, hurting for me, encouraging me, texting notes of support, emails of hope, calls with sympathy, get well wishes. Like I said, standing guard at the door of my room, beside me in the OR, holding me up in recovery, allowing me to sleep when you could not, allowing me to just breathe when you were holding yours that I might live.

It seems to me that each of you had a different assignment, and I am particularly thankful to those of you assigned to hold and comfort the donor and his family. Huge.

Since all of you apparently volunteered for this assignment you might already know this. I think buried in the pile of discharge papers was some fine-print wording that also vested in each of you the duty to hold me accountable for the gift of life. I have an obligation to each of you and particularly the donor to be a good steward of the new heart. Please hold me to that promise.

Forever grateful,

ed

[*Song #5.* Attached to this email was a link to "The Air That I Breathe" by The Hollies.]

Atrial fibrillation (afib): An abnormal heart rhythm. It might begin as brief periods of abnormal, rapid heartbeats that become longer over time. It is a form of supraventricular tachycardia. Treatment for afib can include medications, electrical cardioversion, or ablation.

From: Lisa Mink
Sent: Saturday, July 11, 2015 8:55 PM
Subject: Re: NEW DAY NINE

Ed, you have a wonderful way with words, which speak to how grateful you are for all the love, support, and encouragement you've received on this journey.

But make no mistake about it, your journey has just begun . . .

Hope all is well. I am on call this weekend if you have any questions or concerns.

Lisa

From: Winsome McIntosh
Sent: Sunday, July 12, 2015 2:36 PM
Subject: Re: NEW DAY NINE

Ed,

Two words: Well Done. You need to recognize that your love, determination, will, spirit, and faith enabled your doctors to do their job with stellar results. And your "better half" still wants and needs you in her life as well. That kind of strong love and support is all you needed to help you through the hard part. Now rehab could get a little "testy" as you tire of the constant attention and focus on YOU. Just remember to listen to your "better half" and do what she says. She is and will always be your greatest advocate. Again, Well Done. And with much love . . .

From: Ed Innerarity
Sent: Sunday, July 12, 2015
Subject: Re: NEW DAY NINE

Winsome,

I have been a bit busy lately and am sorry for the delay but I wanted to say how much I admired Mike and how much I will selfishly miss him. [Mike McIntosh, who had recently passed away, owned the Boat Company in Alaska and, along with his wife, Winsome, made sure each passenger on their adventure cruise not only had a great time salmon fishing or whale watching but received a healthy dose of environmental stewardship.] But more than that, he and I are not the same age, we saw each other only yearly, we had as many things that were different about us as we had in common. Mike did his thing there in Washington [In the off-season, Mike lived in DC to be able to monitor any legislation affecting his beloved wild Alaska] and here we are in Midland or Colorado, but here is what I can't seem to figure out. How is it that with only a limited overlap of his life and mine he has made such a profound and permanent impression on me? I once said that if you fished with someone, things were never the same because of the bond the fishing creates. I know we both love the beauty of unspoiled wilderness, but how is it that in less than eight years Mike has left this Alaska-shaped tattoo on my soul? I cannot explain the feeling. I am fortunate to have spent way more than my share of time in the Sierras or waking up in a tent next to some stream, or that some of my favorite possessions are an REI backpack and a magic fly rod that connects me to you and Mike and everyone else I was lucky enough to have spent time with on the river. Perhaps that feeling is best summed up by saying that there are things about Mike that I have adopted as my own and have made part of me—like using that piece of special colored glass that was Mike in the mosaic that is me.

I was honored and blessed to know him and to call him my friend.

ed

From: Ed Innerarity
Sent: Tuesday, July 21, 2015 4:32 PM
Subject: DAY NINETEEN—HOSPITAL SOCKS

Dear Team,

It should come as no surprise, but during this process I set some goals, things I wanted in my life again. Mile markers if you will. Once you pass that mile marker, it has become a milestone of sorts. Obviously, goal numero uno was to stay alive long enough for a heart to be found. Check. No use looking back at that one but on to the next. To me, it's like passing a mile marker on the highway. Good information to have but once you pass it, it does no good to look at it in the rearview mirror because the backsides of mile markers are blank. Same with met goals. On to the next. For me that was breathing on my own, then a good initial biopsy, then enduring the first course of anti-rejection meds. Check, check, and check.

Today I reached another of my goals: to survive as long as Louis Washkansky, the recipient of the first human-to-human heart transplant. Maybe not a significant milestone, but as I have taught my girls: "aim small, miss small." Medicine has come a long way in this field—thanks, Dr. Barnard; thanks, Louis. I have many more goals that I hope to achieve and turn into little personal milestones.

Paige and I made a quick and unannounced trip to Midland this past weekend. It was sort of symbolic that we took the first load of stuff back home. I also surprised the golf group by showing up Saturday morning to "join them." Of course I can't actually play golf for several more weeks so as not to delay the healing of where they butterflied me like a shrimp. I was able to putt a few balls when they were on the green, and in the process, I managed to ruin their rounds. All of them. Oh well. I have learned that if Lazarus is in your foursome, you won't be breaking the course record. Anyway, to my golf buddies: thanks for all the love.

Back to the hospital socks. Once a novelty (I think I got my first pair when I had my knee replaced), now I have a drawer full. The tan ones (from St. David's Hospital) represent all the effort that David and Javier did for the past 10 years. I got a pair of hospital socks when I was shocked out of afib. Another when they implanted the turbo-charged pacemaker in January. And another pair for the fateful echocardiogram that plainly spelled out my options, or rather, the lack thereof.

But the gray ones, issued military style at Seton Hospital, represent the final chapter of everything that led up to the transplant—my second chance and my only hope.

They come neatly packaged as a simple, elegant pair of Pillow Paws®. I would like to think that I am through getting hospital socks for a while. Rejection is not a matter of if, but when. I have been told to expect a rejection episode at some point and meds will be adjusted to deal with that when it comes. Right now my goals are to gain back some weight, work hard at rehab to regain strength, get to drive again, and string together additional biopsies with no meaningful rejection.

Live well, and please sign up to be an organ donor if you are not already.

ed

P.S. I have been asked what's with the music linked to recent emails. It helps. Helps me and seems to frame the thoughts I struggle to express with music I grew up on and made my girls listen to. It is actually fun trying to fit the right song, but the best part is, it doesn't have to have anything to do with my thoughts of the day to still be enjoyable. R.I.P. Sir George.

[*Song #6*. Attached to this email was a link to "Here Comes the Sun" by The Beatles.]

From: Paige Innerarity
Sent: Thursday, July 23, 2015 8:38 PM
Subject: Hitting A Lick For Normalcy

Dear All,

After over eight months of twists and turns, thrills and spills, agony and ecstasy, we seem to be (dare I say it?) hitting a relatively smooth patch in this River of Life. Ed had a really easy time with his third biopsy yesterday. He was calm, the procedure went smoothly, and today, we learned that his rejection numbers were zeroes across the board. We are ecstatic. One more week of good numbers and he will only have biopsies every other week. His medicines are being tweaked weekly, depending on blood work, and the dosages are going down on steroids, in particular. Anti-rejection meds have some particularly unpleasant side effects, so lower doses are always calls for celebration. Cardiac rehab is a high point of the day, always. Ed walks to the hospital, works out, walks home, and is pleasantly fatigued and proud of his accomplishments that day. For a physically active guy, it gets him back to feeling normal, to being himself. Losing his strength, losing the ability to even walk across the street without gasping for breath was terrible for him and for all of us who love him. What a joy to watch him coming back to himself and to us!

As Ed begins hitting his stride again, I see our family doing the same. Everyone is back in their places, "with bright shining faces," living their lives. As parents, nothing is more gratifying than seeing children striving, succeeding, working, and playing hard. We are settling back into life and are so glad we can do so.

So are things "back to normal"? Well, I have to say that I hope things will never be the same as before November 1, 2014, when our lives changed dramatically and, in some ways, forever. Ed faced his own mortality and we faced the prospect of losing him. Through a chain of events that had absolutely nothing to do with our abilities, intelligence, efforts, desires, or control, Ed received a new heart, a miraculous extension of life. I pray each and every day and night that we appreciate this extra time with every breath, every minute we are allowed to hang out on this beautiful, blue marble with the precious saints who grace our lives on this side of heaven.

Life is so fleeting, precious, and beautiful. How dare we not appreciate it?

Love and Grace,
Paige

~~~~~~~~

From: Ed Innerarity
Sent: Thursday, July 23, 2015 9:34 PM
Subject: NEW DAY TWENTY-TWO—JOY IS WHERE YOU MIGHT NOT EXPECT TO FIND IT

To all,

I know I wrote only a couple of days ago, but we got some really good news today; the results of Wednesday's biopsy came back with no rejection! There will be setbacks along this long road to recovery and I will be on certain meds forever. But the news today really buoyed my spirits and those of sweet Paige. The medications (and there are many) are each designed to deal with a specific post-transplant issue. And these can be very big issues. These prescriptions also have significant side effects and interactions among themselves. All of which must be coordinated like Leonard Bernstein in front of the New York Philharmonic. There is always the risk of becoming diabetic or developing kidney problems, I will become more prone to sun and skin issues, and lots of others. I will find a way to handle that. I am managing to deal with the side effects, although it is not always pretty. At times my hands are as shaky as the Greek economy. Bring it on. I am anemic because I am not handling the iron supplement, so I am trying to make that up with foods rich in iron that are on my ok to eat list: spinach, hazelnuts, octopus. I can do that, too.

About the biopsies: They enter the jugular vein or something important like that in my neck and, with a long medical thing, run down and around the heart and then they take small samples of my new heart to look for signs of rejection. Doing the biopsy is none other than Dr. Cishek herself. I was told she had done 10,000 such biopsies, or as I told her Wednesday, she is up to 10,003, because I am pretty sure right now I am her only patient. I am adequately sedated (but awake) and in the very best of hands, but I won't pretend; I am not brave about this. Not brave, not one bit. But I can do this too, and when the results come back like today, it is all worth it. There is some more of that joy, down there in that vein.

Here is more joy—my post op rehab workouts. I make a game of trying to get up, fix breakfast, and get off to rehab without waking Paige. She has really been through it, so for her to not have to fix me breakfast or take me to the hospital is another bit of joy. It is only four or five blocks, but I feel like Andy Dufresne after breaking out of Shawshank and the 10-minute walk is truly liberating. I can't ride my bike because it would put too much strain on my recently parted sternum. The walk back is more like a trudge, but I can do that, too.

About the rehab: Before the surgery, before the call, I was working out to improve my surgical odds and increase the chances of lasting until the call came. But the post-op rehab is for my new life. To make the most of each bonus-life day. I owe it to myself. And to my family. And to my untold prayer warriors. And I owe it to the donor and his family. There is some more of that joy, over there by the treadmill.

There is joy for me in simple promises I made that if I survived, I was going to buy all new stuff. All new socks, all new underwear, new jeans, all new golf shirts (just like Jordan Spieth's, I might add), new golf shorts, new workout shoes. You get the point. Some of this was out of practicality since I now weigh what I weighed in college, most of it is a slightly extravagant gift to my second shot at getting it right.

Live well, and thanks to those of you who just became organ donors.

(While finishing this email, I just got Paige's update. Talk about bad timing; that is a tough act to follow. I guess you can tell how excited we are about the biopsy news. Hard to hold that in. Anyway, sorry for any duplication, at least mine has music.)

ed

About the music: The song came out at the same time Paige and I got married and of course we made the girls listen to it. During this heart ordeal, I learned from Sarah that she considered it to be our song, I guess because I played it so often on trips.

You may find it interesting to know that the signature pedal steel guitar that frames the song was played by none other than Jerry Garcia. Grateful for the music, Jerry.

[*Song #7*. Attached to this email was a link to "Teach Your Children" by Crosby, Stills & Nash.]

From: David Koch
Sent: Saturday, July 25, 2015 7:41 PM
Subject: Re: NEW DAY TWENTY-TWO—JOY IS WHERE YOU MIGHT NOT EXPECT TO FIND IT

Ed,

I came home from work yesterday . . . clicked on the TV and within 10 seconds a Neil Young concert was on U-Verse . . . (I'm not smart enough to know what channel, but I hit the record button)—the first song I heard was "Heart of Gold" . . . so I just closed my eyes and listened . . . may God bless your heart and fill it with courage . . . thanks to you and Paige and all your family for the privilege of what you all have shared with us . . . your actions, your words, your meditations, and your spirit . . . they are all gifts to all of us . . . my brother.

From: Ed Innerarity
Sent: Friday, July 31, 2015 4:34 AM
Subject: **Day Twenty-Nine: Going Home**

"Climb the mountains and get their good tidings."

—JOHN MUIR

Team:

My transplant took place in the very early morning of July 2 (even though we had gotten the call the morning before). It was a full moon that day. Now, 29 days later, July 31st, and four very important biopsies later, we are headed home. Today is also a full moon, in fact a blue moon. Something symmetrical about that. (Curiously enough, there was a full moon in June, a Strawberry Moon, on June 2nd, our anniversary.)

This week's biopsy came back with a zero, meaning no rejection. Very good news for many reasons including slight downward adjustments in some meds. We are not so much going home but getting a nice break from Austin and the folks we have come to love at Seton to run up to the cabin in Colorado for a few days. The all-important biopsies are now every other week, giving us (and especially Paige) a chance to spend a few precious days at our place in Creede. It will be almost a year since we were last there. And what a year it has been.

I had some rich and clever things I was going to say about the symbolism of leaving empty coat hangers behind in the apartment, but I found out yesterday that I could write a letter to the donor family. We have a winner! I thought it would be a year, but they said I could write it provided that I not give my full name and not mention the transplant center, all for the sake of the donor's feelings. Maybe they will read my letter, maybe not. They might reply, might not. At least I get to put on paper what this has meant for me and how I might spend the new life afforded by the donor's selfless act. I only wish that my already bad handwriting was not made worse by the trembling in my hands from the various meds. I hope they can see my thoughts even if they can't read all the words.

And more good news: two other guys in my "transplant class" got new hearts this past Thursday. And a third one yesterday. Only one of them I actually knew from rehab, and it was such a joy to see my prayers answered for this guy who had worked so hard. He had really struggled at times. His condition several months ago had gotten so bad that he was given a heart mate, a battery powered heart-assisting pump. This moved him to an inactive status on the waiting list for six months, to provide time to heal. After six months, he was back on the waiting list, with credit for "prior days on list." And now he has a new heart and the pump is gone. The two guys were both five days post-transplant when I got to see them on Tuesday. Now they have this same second chance in life; very special to see, very special to experience, very special to be a part of.

And the most recent good news came Thursday afternoon when Paige and I met with the surgeon who did the actual transplant. I met him briefly just minutes before he went to work sawing me in half. I was about half cooked with the pre-op cocktails, but I remember holding a picture of me fly fishing in Alaska on my chest right over my tired, barely beating, worn out heart. In the picture, I had a salmon on the line and the guide took the shot over my shoulder with a bear coming across the stream hoping for some hors d'oeuvres. It was raining, I was grinning and the guide was worried. I told Dr. Kirkland I wanted him to help me get back there. At today's appointment, he said he remembered that conversation and might want to go with me. Perhaps, more importantly, I got an across-the-board good check-up. Heart is strong; sternum healing is solid, OK to drive some, OK to fly fish. Some things I will need to wait for, but a very good report.

I am a very blessed guy. A million things could have gone wrong. Lots of things still can, and the journey is really just beginning. I was forcibly moved out of my comfort zone. Almost everything important was taken away. I had to move out of town and let people do things to me that I don't like. All that was just to make the transplant list. I had to wait and wait. I lost sense of time. And wondered—might I die, might I have a stroke, and even though it is the only viable option to keep me alive, how can I possibly face the surgery and the biggest battle of my life? Like I said, I am a very blessed guy. And everyone around me has been wonderful.

Live well, like you might not live forever.

ed

About the music. Everyone likes this John Denver song, even though we are going to Colorado, not West Virginia. I have never even been to West Virginia. In fact, the guy that co-wrote the original version of this song had never been to the Mountaineer State before the song was written. But it is a great going home song. And of course we made our girls listen to it, too.

The Marcels' hit was too obvious not to include, although written in the '30s.

[*Songs #8 and #9.* Attached to this email were links to "Take Me Home, Country Roads" by John Denver and "Blue Moon" by The Marcels.]

From: Ed Innerarity
Sent: Sunday, August 2, 2015 8:27 AM
Subject: ANY QUESTIONS?

"In our family, there was no clear line between religion and fly fishing. We lived at the junction of great trout rivers in western Montana, and our father was a Presbyterian minister and a fly fisherman who tied his own flies and taught others. He told us about Christ's disciples being fishermen, and we were left to assume, as my brother and I did, that all first-class fishermen on the Sea of Galilee were fly fishermen and that John, the favorite, was a dry-fly fisherman."

—Norman Maclean, *A River Runs Through It*

Live well,

ed

Today's song is "The Road to Ensenada" by Lyle Lovett.

[*Song #10.* Attached to this email was a link to "The Road to Ensenada" by Lyle Lovett.]

From: Caroline Cowden
Sent: Sunday, August 2, 2015 8:27 AM
Subject: Re: ANY QUESTIONS?

Hallelujah, praise God from whom all blessings flow . . . like the river!!!!

From: Ed Innerarity
Sent: Sunday, August 2, 2015 9:23 PM
Subject: One month today

Today, I took my new heart fly fishing. It learned quickly.

From: David Terreson
Sent: Monday, August 3, 2015 5:39 AM
Subject: Re: ANY QUESTIONS?

That picture pretty much sums it up.
    Probably the best opening sentence for a book, ever.

David

From: Mark Leaverton
Sent: Sunday, August 9, 2015 6:46 PM
Subject: Thinking of You

We are sitting here eating a P. Terry's burger and we are talking about you. Hoping you are continuing to heal and get back to a wonderfully normal life. How are you doing? Can you have visitors yet? Love to you and Paige.

Heart transplants are not for the weak or cowardly. God has been so good to you and because of your humility and attitude toward all this, you, too, have done your very best in dealing with all these ups and downs. I cannot begin to imagine what you are going through. Nobody I know has ever dealt with anything like this. Needless to say, we will be praying today as you get biopsy #6 and for all those little white guys to really get excited and multiply like crazy. One of your most cherished blessings is Paige. I don't know the load she has carried and the difficulties she has faced all the while uplifting and encouraging you. None of us would have in our wildest imaginations thought you and Paige would be going down this path. It is a day-to-day walk and a day-to-day, maybe hour-to-hour, trust that God is in control and has the perfect plan for you and Paige. I love that when you hurt you think of the donor and the donor's family. That is very honoring to them and to the Lord who gave you this new life. You will get better and you will fly fish again and love on your grandchildren! Keep us posted. You know how much we love our dearest friend.

Mark Leaverton

From: Ed Innerarity
Sent: Tuesday, August 11, 2015 11:57 PM
Subject: DAY FORTY

Team,

If any of you happen to see or hear from Paige, please pass along my thanks for driving us home after the biopsy today. And for all the other times she had to drive because I had just had surgery.

And you might want to thank her for all the meals she cooked when I could not or would not eat anything but something she fixed. No pressure there. And for sharing a 602 sq. ft. apartment, which includes my bicycle (which I rode every day to rehab and to the grocery store), my drone (which I am now on my fourth, two are in the lake behind the apartment, but don't ask), and my golf clubs (which I never got to use in Austin because the day after I brought them with me I got a new heart. Oh well). 602 square feet and no place to hide, no place to run. Yeah, thanks.

Oh, and someone might want to say thanks for being the main chef required to come up with more menu ideas than the Disney Cruise Line. And right now too, please. And when we did go out, Paige never got to pick where we went out, always deferred to my fickle taste buds and random appetite. OK, so thanks for that. Did I mention how many twice-baked potatoes she fixed me?

But how do you say thanks to someone who had to watch as I was slowly dying, which is way worse than slowly dying yourself. Do you send a thank-you note? A card?

Someone needs to give Paige a pat on the back for the endless conferences with doctors, nurses, pharmacists, hospital staff, and home health-care workers regarding all the medical supplies and prescriptions, and for all the sterile heart juice changes. (For which I was always a good sport.)

Few doctor visits, hospital stays, or trips to the ICU make me fun to be with and sweet Paige had to put up with all of that and more. I have learned that when you are dying, you don't make the best dinner companion. And that when you are hurting, you aren't the most fun to be around. And that when you are so scared about a pending procedure that you are shaking for two days before, you are not good company. Ditto for when the medications make you crazy. Ditto for when you cannot sleep. Ditto when it seems a heart will never be found. Double ditto for having to turn almost completely inward to prepare for the battle of my life. I am guessing that all of this is less fun for Paige than hiking with Babe in the mountains right before the rain hits. I am also guessing that all of this is less fun than having a root canal in Juarez, Mexico. On a Friday afternoon. During the World Cup! I need to somehow say thanks for putting up with all that. Somehow. Yes, a card for sure.

Oh, and one of us needs to tell her thanks for walking that impossibly thin line of keeping the girls informed of what is going on but never letting them get discouraged by the news. Being accurate but always leaving room for hope, however bad it really was, however desperate the news or the situation really was. Always holding it together for the girls. Never letting me see how scared she really was. Always patient with me no matter how many days in a row I felt bad or how worn out I was every evening. Every one of them. Every single one.

I learned something in the last day or two I did not know before. It is no secret to anyone that was around me the last nine months that few things comforted me like ice chips. By lunchtime most days, I was crunching on ice chips (the ice at Sonic was just right, not too soft, not too hard). The dentist told me it was not good long term, but he did not finish his sentence. Since a few days after my transplant, I no longer have the desire to crunch on ice. I just learned from Paige that in the last weeks of my mother's life, she (Paige) made many a trip to the Racquet Club for ice chips for Mother. Paige fed them to her as she rapidly approached the end of her life. Until this week, I was spared that story. Paige was concerned I would connect the dots and project my problems into my mother's fatal trajectory, which I probably would have. Only many weeks after the transplant did Paige share that story, sparing me again from more anxiety. Maybe one of us could tell her thanks for that too.

When she did have free time, when I would ride my bike to rehab for the morning or for clinic, Paige rewarded herself by doing all the linens and trying to keep the apartment as clean and germ free as possible. That is how I want to spend my free time for sure.

Paige was all the time getting food and snack platters for the ICU nurses. Always thanking each of them for taking such good care of me. And all this time, I thought they just enjoyed my wit and sense of humor.

I learned this after the fact as well: On January 2nd of this year, my electrophysiologist implanted a new super duper pacemaker and coffee maker all-in-one. It could do it all. I was in recovery and the doctor, whom we think the world of, told Paige that he "hoped the new device would help, but based on some testing he did during the surgery, he had his doubts . . . We would know for sure within a couple of weeks." Paige began to cry, only to have the doctor, still in surgical scrubs, warn her not to let me see her like this and not to say anything, just yet. Yeah, hold that information like battery acid so I don't get rattled any more than I am already.

Most of the IV lines and PICC lines were installed in my ICU room and poor Paige frequently had to witness first-hand when much of that did not go smoothly. I was being protected and lifted up and spared from most of the "not fun medical stuff." And I know many of you were lifting her up too and protecting her too, but she had to see someone she cared about go through things she knew I would not enjoy and could not possibly handle. Please pass along my thanks for that too.

She remembered all the names I could not; she remembered to ask all the questions I seemed to forget; she went over all the options with me when I was firing on fewer than all cylinders. On more than one occasion, I was presented with a difficult decision on a particularly tough procedure. I was so overwhelmed I could not focus on even this one important issue. I remember turning to Paige and asking her to make the decision for me. She did, and it worked out. I need to say thanks for that too. I am not sure what being the one named on the Medical Power of Attorney, with "plug pulling responsibilities," is like spending a week at that spa outside of Tucson. Not quite.

I am happy to report that biopsy #6 is in the books. We know this is just the beginning of the post-transplant journey, and there will be bumps along the way. But for now, we rejoice and give thanks for 40 days that I might not have had before and ask for the vision and wisdom to make the most of every bonus day.

Live well, like you really love someone.

ed

From: Caroline Cowden
Sent: Friday, August 14, 2015 10:58 AM
Subject: Re: DAY FORTY

No words can describe your precious wife!!!! Your number one angel for sure!!!! What a testimony for how much she loves you no matter what! Ed, you also did all of those things for Paige when she had her wreck and miraculously lived through it! She was truly amazing through many surgeries and years of pain! You were her number one angel! What a testimony of how much you love her!!!!! God is SO good and so are you and Paige! It was an honor and privilege to watch you both battle through these journeys with such faith and grace!!! I love you both SO much!!!! Praise God for the victorious outcome!!!!!

Caroline

From: Ed Innerarity
Sent: Thursday, August 20, 2015 3:53 AM
Subject: K-T BOUNDARY

Fellow hurdlers,

Just over 65 million years ago, a meteor seven miles across slammed into Earth just off the coast of present-day Yucatán Peninsula. It punched a hole nearly 20 miles into the Earth. This was a major geologic event and was "discovered" just as I was getting into the oil business. The Chicxulub impact resulted in extensive plant and animal extinction, including the dinosaurs. Since I consider myself to be an earth scientist, I have been intrigued by an event so global that it marked the boundary between the Cretaceous and Tertiary periods and is widely referred to as the *K-T Boundary*. The impact sent huge quantities of the distinctive shocked quartz around the earth. Today, the layered, shocked quartz and associated iridium outcrops are found in several places around the world. I have wanted to see one of those outcrops and now that I have new ventricles, I decided that now is the time. So after this morning's trip to Del Norte for lab work, I drove on over to Trinidad, Colorado, where the K-T Boundary shows itself. On the drive back, I was thinking about boundaries, geologic and otherwise.

Funny thing about boundaries, they don't have to be limitations, maybe they are well-camouflaged opportunities. Thinly disguised new beginnings. The K-T event was not so good for T-Rex and his scaly friends yet the earth became a mostly blank sheet of paper for what came next. The Alps and the Himalayas were next, and more. Much more. Two summers ago the mountains between Creede, South Fork, and Pagosa Springs were on fire for weeks. One of the largest wildfires ever in the state. This on top of a massive tree die-off over the past decade from the pine beetle. The combination was bad. Paige and I will not live to see the old forests return to the mountains behind Creede, but our grand-daughter will. And in the meantime, change and new life and different trees and new beginnings take their place. Two years ago the Forest Service placed a boundary around the area to hikers and backpackers. The Rio Grande was black for months with ash from the fire. But inside that boundary today is new life. Different to be sure, but new and fresh and very much alive. The ash in fact was the best fertilizer for the valley, and the fish are back as before.

Makes you wonder about other life-changing events that we can easily treat like boundaries: That first job we are not wild about. Is it a boundary or an opportunity? An important class with a prof that I could not stand. A new marriage about to be embarked on. An unappreciative boss. Taking a chance on a career change. An illness. Adding to the family. Moving, because of opportunity or lack thereof. Going to (different kinds of) rehab with hopes of being better, stronger, different, changed. Being alone after the loss of a loved one. Seeing our children and grandchildren off to college. Watching our loved ones age and die. What to make of a new person in your life? Our own fears. Again, boundary or opportunity?

I cannot speak for anyone else, but in my life I remember seeing in the distance what were surely insurmountable obstacles. As they came closer, they still seemed overwhelming. The end of the high diving board, making the team, Dr. Ashby in graduate school, a boss I could not please, trying to make a living in 1986 with $10 per barrel, my own stubbornness. Through grace, and maybe some hard work, I made it over, around, or through those barriers, and once overcome, they became very important life lessons. I learned perseverance, tact, and maybe even some patience.

Maybe the boundaries in our lives we put there ourselves. I know I do. About nine months ago, when things first started to head south for me medically, I had three different doctors mention a transplant as a possible option. No thank you, no thanks, thanks but no. Not for me, I can beat this heart thing. Anyway, I knew first-hand the possibility of a stroke, and that was a deal breaker. And right there I built a 10-foot-tall boundary. No transplant, no way, no how. But, about five or six months ago, I had a very frank conversation with Rebecca. I think I was at the farm. We were having dinner together like we often do at the end of a long, hard, productive day, and I asked her what she thought of me maybe getting a heart transplant. She said except for the stroke risk, it might be worth doing. Look at how we all would benefit if it worked. And except for the stroke thing, what's the worst that can happen? I die and am in heaven. So we decided on a plan to deal with a bad stroke, discussed it with the whole family over Easter, and the boundary I created was dismantled and the many fine folks at Seton went to work. I am pretty sure I was their only "needs-a-heart" patient, at least it seemed that way.

Easy to say for the guy with the new heart. Maybe. Maybe not. I don't know why I got this heart; others needed it just as much or more. I don't know why I got this second chance either. Make no mistake about it; my medical battles are certainly not over. I will be on some of these meds for the rest of my life. There will be things I cannot do again, boundaries of a sort to be sure. But for each of those, a dozen new beginnings, new adventures, new perspectives, new priorities.

Paige and I have been away from our friends in Midland for many months now. Austin was a necessity, and Creede is an important place for Paige to get a breather and for me to gather myself and prepare for life again. Many friends who have not seen me ask, "How are you doing, really?" I am doing great. I get up early and fix my own breakfast, update my spreadsheets on medications, weight, calorie intake, etc. I am working to get completely off the pain medications, but some days it still hurts where they sawed me in half. OK, I learn something from the pain; I don't celebrate it, but I try and learn. I very much need to gain back some weight. From last November 1, I have lost 31 pounds. The weight is slowly coming back, and with it some perspective: There are others out there, Ed, that struggle and hurt way more than you ever did. Maybe you better think about that. I am trying to regain strength and some semblance of muscle mass. Hard to do too much because of the parting of the sternum, but the strength is slowly coming back. I can actually open a pickle jar for Paige. And with the strength in my hands and arms and legs, it seems like I am getting wisdom about things I might have paid more attention to the past 63 years.

I tried real hard for many years to teach our girls to be all they could. I would tell them they could do anything. Now I am trying to learn that lesson, again.

No boundaries.

Live well, like a meteor is coming.

ed

"I like geography best, he said, because your mountains
& rivers know the secret. Pay no attention to boundaries."
—BRIAN ANDREAS

[*Song #11*. Attached to this email was a link to "How Can You Mend a Broken Heart" by the Bee Gees.]

From: Ed Innerarity
Sent: Thursday, August 20, 2015 7:12 PM
Subject: K-T BOUNDARY UPDATE

No known connection, but shortly after I was at the K-T boundary site yesterday with my trusty rock hammer, there was a 4.2 earthquake at the same locale. I had suspected that when we mess with life's boundaries, things get shaken up a bit. Maybe more than a bit. Of course, it was probably just a coincidence.

Live well, like we might shake things up.

ed

From: Joe Gifford
Sent: Monday, August 24, 2015 3:15 PM
Subject: Re: K-T BOUNDARY

Dear Ed —

Well, oil hit $35 per barrel posted today and the "experts" say that this may not be the bottom. But you need not worry because, after reading your unique epistles, you certainly have potential as a best-selling author. I was fascinated by your knowledge of the K-T boundary separating the Cretaceous and the Tertiary. Since you have gone in search of this boundary in the rocks, which tell us the complete history of the earth, you would be fascinated by the book *Earth in Upheaval* by Immanuel Velikovsky (available at Amazon) that I picked up in a corner bookstore next to our apartment in Paris in 1962. Would that all of the global warming nuts could read this! I met with our Bishop last week with several other oil people to talk about the Pope's encyclical on global warming. I was able to get some things off my chest, which helped my atrial fibrillation. So glad to hear that things are going well health wise for you and that you and Paige are not here enjoying our 104 degree days.

Joe

From: Pam Stoltz
Sent: Thursday, August 20, 2015 8:15 PM
Subject: Re: K-T BOUNDARY

Like a meteor's coming . . . I'm gonna remember that.

From: Lisa Mink
Sent: Thursday, August 20, 2015 9:26 PM
Subject: Re: K-T BOUNDARY

One of the best reads so far. Loved it!!!!

Lisa

From: Paige Innerarity
Sent: Thursday, August 20, 2015 10:27 PM
Subject: NATURAL LIGHT

Dear All,

Leaving behind the heat of Texas for the mountains and water of southern Colorado seemed like a really good time to give you all (and myself) a break from emails. As much as I enjoy writing, I find myself feeling self-conscious about sharing what is going on with us post-transplant. When does sharing become over-sharing? I shudder to think that I am guilty of that! Anyway, I did have some thoughts hit me gently between the eyes when I was hiking with Babe today that I wanted to tap out.

I have always been a fan of natural light. The houses we have lived in over the years usually had big windows, skylights, and minimum window treatments. One of the first things we did with our cabin in Colorado was to have the tiny windows removed. Next, in a rather dramatic fashion, larger holes were chain-sawed in the logs so that we could have big windows and "Let the Sunshine In." We raised the ceilings, the walls were slathered with a vanilla bean shade of plaster, and our cabin was filled with glorious, natural light. It makes me happy. It makes me calm. My attitude lightens, and I can think more clearly and see more clearly.

One of the very best things about being in the mountains is watching the light change during the day. Clouds and trees and even the time of year change the natural light. Walking in a stand of aspen trees is entirely different from walking in a high meadow or a forest of spruce trees. Morning light is nothing like the afternoon. Ed can tell you that the light has a profound effect on the fishing, and why. I don't know about that, really. I just know I love to watch the changes during the day, the week, the season—it fascinates me!

Since November 1st, our family has undergone profound change. Sometimes, it seemed like we were shaken up in a Yahtzee dice cup and thrown on a board in a new configuration every few hours. There is no natural light in that dice cup. There is precious little natural light in most hospitals and doctors' offices. Ed and I did find a fifth-floor patio at Seton where we could be outside while he was still in intensive care. We spent lots of time there.

So, what is my point? I guess I am saying that for me, for those I love, maybe for most people, I highly recommend getting outside to be your best self. My children can attest to my belief (because they have heard me espousing it FOREVER) that playing outside and drinking plenty of water will pretty much clear the mental cobwebs and go a long way in settling one's emotions.

Of course, a new heart was necessary for Ed, as well as proper hydration and sunshine. Medicine, ongoing medical procedures, and monitoring are part of his life forever, and we are grateful for the miracles that have been achieved by the dedicated pioneers of research in heart disease and transplant. But, how wonderful to see this man who was dying before my eyes restored to health, to the life he loves! I can see him so clearly in this place that is a spiritual stronghold for our family, in the natural light.

Love and Grace,
Paige

From: Ed Innerarity
Sent: Tuesday, September 1, 2015 9:46 PM
Subject: PATIENT'S BELONGINGS

Team,

On most of my surgical trips and for every biopsy, the routine is similar. After check-in, I am escorted back to the pre-op place and asked to put on a hospital gown, and I am given a bag to put my clothes in. I get the clothes back afterward. My clothes, my bag. In fact, the amply sized plastic bag is clearly labeled (in reassuring hospital blue) PATIENT'S BELONGINGS. Not that anyone should want my dedicated hospital sneakers or my lucky golf shirt. I have collected several such bags. Back to the Patient's Belongings bag later.

Today is opening day of dove season in Texas. I am one day short of 60 days post-transplant. My cardiothoracic surgeon, Dr. Hunter Kirkland, was at first reluctant to allow me to hunt birds this soon after the chest sawing. Something about the repeated firing and recoil that close to the cut area and besides the season opens only 59 days post-op. So I made a deal; I will use the smallest shotgun made (.410 for those of you that know about these things) and light loads and I will stop if anything feels out of place. Deal! The planning begins.

My good friend, Barry Beal, was similarly coerced into inviting me to their place opening day. I was there eight minutes after sun-up. So were thousands of white wings (a very special and desired type of dove). I had also been warned not to handle the birds barehanded and to wear gloves and a mask when cleaning them. Deal. So I wear a work glove on my non-shooting hand, so as Babe brings the birds back I collect them from her in the gloved hand and put them into the sack. The plastic sack. The plastic sack from the hospital for Patient's Belongings. (If necessary, please refer to paragraph 1 above.)

I kind of liked the symmetry of using that same hospital bag for my first limit of doves. And it made me wonder: What are my belongings?? What are yours? I have a .410, and I also have friends. More friends than white-winged doves it seems. I have my lucky "today is biopsy day" golf shirt, and I also have a new heart, a new perspective, and a new dove season. How many of my belongings will fit in that bag? I have three wonderful daughters that are smart and strong-willed and independent, like Paige. I have hope. Is there room in that bag for hope? I have memories of doing lots of fun things with the family and with friends. I have the opportunity to make more memories, with my new heart, my new granddaughter, my great family, and my white-winged abundant friends. Pretty sure we are going to need another bag.

Live well, like you are going to need another bag.

ed

P.S. Paige is trying a new way of cooking doves, on the grill, with fresh jalapeños and heart-healthy bacon.

From: Paige Innerarity
Sent: Tuesday, September 1, 2015 10:30 PM
Subject: Re: PATIENT'S BELONGINGS

Dear All,

I must amend the recipe reference to "heart-healthy bacon." No, it was just good ole thick-cut bacon. I did use just a third of a slice per bird, however.

Love, Grace, and Bacon Always,
Paige

From: Ed Innerarity
Sent: Wednesday, September 16, 2015 7:59 PM
Subject: RECENT HEART TRANSPLANT

Dr. Kirkland,

I am Lloyd Innerarity (11-06-51) and I received a heart transplant on July 2 of this year. We met only minutes before the surgery and again for my 30-day post-op check-up. In a sentence, I am doing great. You allowed me to hunt if I used a .410, which I did. I have regained most of my weight and am working steadily on regaining strength. My seven biopsies (#8 is early next Wednesday) have gone well with almost no rejection.

But more than just an update, I wanted to say thank you. I refuse to accept that I was just another transplant; I felt like the only transplant patient. Many friends ask, and I tell them honestly that after the first few days the pain was very tolerable. You may recall that I had a picture of me fly fishing in Alaska that I wanted to tape on my chest and ask you to help me get back there. Maybe no Alaska yet, but I have been able to fly fish at our place in Colorado.

Not just because things have gone so well thus far, but because I have been entrusted with a fresh heart that came from another man; with your help, I hope to be the best possible host for many years to come.

Again, many thanks.
L. Edward Innerarity, Jr.
Midland, Texas

From: Hunter Kirkland
Sent: Friday, September 18, 2015 1:15 PM
Subject: **Heart Txplant**

Hello Mr. Innerarity,

I just wanted to let you know I'll definitely come meet you. Always very gratifying to have that conversation—I am indescribably pleased that you are doing so well. Why don't you text me when you get to pre-op? It might also serve to get me out of a Transplant Committee meeting . . .

Best Regards,
HQK

[Dr. Kirkland and I did indeed meet as he came by pre-op the following week right as I was being prepped for biopsy #8.]

From: Ed Innerarity
Sent: Sunday, November 8, 2015 6:00 PM
Subject: SURPRISE BIRTHDAY

Friends and Family,

OK, not really a total surprise birthday. But it was a surprise that Brian, Kate, and Niam [our "grandson" from not-official son Brian Batch] showed up. Baron and Caroline also made it. I had been told the Batch men could not make it and Paige's sister has been there every minute of this adventure, so it was extra-special to see her too.

It has been four months since the big event, and we gathered at the Biltmore in Arizona this weekend. We have many things to celebrate, including the birthday we thought I might not have. I turned 64 on Friday: 11-06-51. (At the hospital they have asked me for my date of birth hundreds of times. My correct answer was usually followed by being handed a hospital gown and having something sharp inserted in one of my veins or being asked to lie very still and try to relax.) With any luck, this will be my last such birthday because I am planning on observing my birthday on the day my donor was born. I have been told almost nothing about my donor. Out of respect for the donor's family, they will obviously have all the time they need before I might hear from them. In fact, there is every possibility that they might choose not to meet me at all. But that does not alter the fact that if not for the donor's supreme act of generosity and selflessness, this most certainly would have been my last 11-06-51. All future birthdays, anniversaries, Christmases, Thanksgivings, meteor showers, firework shows, road trips, hay cuttings, rounds of golf, mornings on the river, days on the trail, nights in a tent, time with family, time with friends are possible because of his heart. And because of my fantastic team of professionals at Seton Hospital. And because of all the support I have received from all of you.

We had a great time—wonderful long meals together, two grandchildren, family grudge tennis match, swimming, croquet, family walks, millions of pictures, giant chess on the lawn. But mostly being together and laughing.

My new heart did not come with a guarantee, to be sure; "as is, where is," buyer beware, all sales are final. It is still up to me to be a good host, stay in shape, take my meds, eat right, and stay healthy. I plan to be a good steward of my new heart for many years, but I take each new day as the bonus it really is. I am somewhere between not buying green bananas and planting a pecan orchard to harvest 20 years from now. I am thankful for each new sunrise; while praying for a long and full life for my new heart. Let there be no doubt, I am doing so well that I lean toward the pecan orchard most of the time. I am almost back to what I weighed before and have regained my strength and endurance. I feel like a new person, probably because I am. And I think it is only fitting that my new birthday be celebrated on the birthday of my donor and his heart. Maybe it's my life, but this second chance is due to his heart.

The other reason I think I have done so well is that I had the best family support. The Best. And the most caring and devoted of nurses. The Best. Absolutely the hardest working and skilled doctors. Absolutely. And the most patient of rehab folks. I went to one transplant support group meeting shortly after getting on the waiting list. Next month there is the big annual Christmas meeting. I am really looking forward to it. I hope to see the Romanian guy that got his heart a few weeks before me; he was a very big help in preparing me. I hope to see the others in my transplant "group" who have gotten hearts, are still waiting, or have gotten a mechanical assist device, the external heart pump I call the heart mate. Much to celebrate with them too. Everybody it seems is going to be having a new birthday.

Since just before I went on the transplant list, all of you have indulged me in writing these "updates." Sure, a small part of these really were updates, but mostly they were my best outlet. A way to hurt in front of you, bleed in front of you, and cry in front of you when I couldn't hold it all in. I used all of you as my escape from the fear and the pain. Basically a coward about the medical stuff, I chose the easy way out. I made fun of something serious, I brought you along when I could not face bad news alone, I vented about things none of us have any control over. The journey of a heart transplant recipient and associated medical adventures will last the rest of my life. Just as my biopsies are coming less often, so will these emails. Each of you was so supportive, but time for me to resume "my normal life." Time to turn our thoughts and prayers to others in need. However, if something funny comes up, I will likely share that.

I remember the look on the faces of my family and friends during the really bad days last spring. I was dying and you could read that on their worried and troubled faces. That is why this weekend was so special. But in the same way, I wish I could have brought all of you with us. And all those who prayed for us, many of whom I will never meet. I made it because of all of you. Like I said before, somehow saying thanks just doesn't quite cover it.

Please don't wake up some day and feel like you wasted opportunities along the way.

Live well, like it might be your last birthday.

ed

About the music: "Wasted on the Way" was one of the last big hits by CSN and came out in the early '80s. It is one of the few songs I did not make the girls listen to because at the time, I did not understand what the message really was. FYI, David Crosby sings vocals and plays acoustic guitar on this song. A talented musician, he was a member of the Byrds before CSN. Crosby had numerous personal demons and in 1994, he received a liver transplant.

[*Song #12*. Attached to this email was a link to "Wasted on the Way" by Crosby, Stills & Nash.]

From: Bridget Hyde
Sent: Sunday, November 8, 2015 9:40 PM
Subject: Re: SURPRISE BIRTHDAY

Dear Ed,

I listened to the CSN music before reading your letter and it definitely set the tone. It is astounding to hear that Crosby also found a revived life through organ donation. My heart is truly gladdened by the fun pictures of the gathering around you, and the celebration that shows in each smile. Bravo! All of you are grand to give back in love and joy, and teach the rest of us more and more about the blessings in each moment.

Thank you for sharing the miracle.

Many happy returns to you of sunsets and baby giggles and long tables completely filled with those you love. You are helping me remember that in every day there is birth. Thank you!

With hope,
Bridget

From: Ed Innerarity
Sent: Sunday, November 8, 2015 9:01 PM
To: My golf group
Subject: BIRTHDAY TRIP BONUS

Guys,

In celebration of my b'day and everything else, we brought the whole clan to the Biltmore in Arizona. Knowing I would not have time to play golf, I did not bring my clubs.

The second day here I noticed something going on at the golf course. It was the Fiesta Bowl hole-in-one contest. The closest shot to the pin each of the next seven days or any hole(s) in one goes to the finals next Sunday for a shot at $1MM. Wells Fargo was the big sponsor.

I had to try. So when everyone was resting I went over to give it a shot. They had some Ping [golf club] demos so I was ready. I signed up and waited my turn. The "golfers" hit off AstroTurf on a raised platform with room for 20 golfers at a time. They had 10 spotters behind a wall up by the green. Any ball that bounced off another ball and went in did not count. If someone hit one close, play was stopped and a measurement was taken. At the same time, they raked the green clean. If there was a hole in one, play was stopped, the ball retrieved, and the golfer station number was announced. Hitting into a clean green, that golfer hit a validation ball to serve as a tiebreaker.

When they called for a halt because of a hole in one this morning, I did not know it was mine, although I already had a 3'3" shot and another that was 1'1". I was the closest to the flag at that point. Other guys had close ones too. Then they called out #17. By the time the green was cleared off and they brought me the ball, I was in no shape to hit a validation ball. I think I missed the green. But it did not matter; I was automatically in the finals next Sunday for the $1MM try. All holes-in-one advance, or if none that day, whoever was closest. I think they said I had the only one today, but yesterday they had two or three when the flag was up front. Those 8–10 guys get one try each for the big money. There are also other day prizes. I got a new set of Ping irons and some other stuff. The winner and the closest five get to go to the Fiesta Bowl. I don't think Texas will be there this year. At the game they give the winner a check the size and shape of South Dakota.

The pin was 128 yards away and I hit a Ping wedge from the demo bag. I win $5 from each of you, less the $6 I still owe Grant. Lots of fun. Nice to be back in the game again.

ed

From: Paige Innerarity
Sent: Tuesday, December 1, 2015
Subject: Choices and Chance

One of the surprises for Ed's birthday weekend was a beautiful book that our daughter Laura Paige compiled and edited of letters, memories, and pictures from some of our family and friends. It is a treasure. Some memories are poignant, some are very funny, all are important because they were written with intention. I told the children that Ed must feel like Tom Sawyer when he attended his own funeral and realized how many people cared about him! I don't think it is appropriate for me to share the thoughts and stories of others without their "express written permission" so I am just sending what I wrote.

Choices and Chance

Sometimes, our lives seem so random, so utterly ruled by chance. Other times, we seem to be walking a path that was mapped for us since birth. I have never subscribed to the theory that life is a series of accidents, coincidences, and luck. My faith gives me the certainty that I am here for a specific purpose, that my decisions and choices are important. Because I believe that to be true for myself, I believe the same holds true for everyone. Nowhere, in no life, have I seen that as clearly as I see it in your life, Ed.

You have been preparing your entire life to receive this precious gift of a new heart. From having polio, and overcoming it as a small boy, you have been preparing to face the incredible obstacles of heart disease and a second chance at life. You recovered from polio, you became a highly ranked junior swimmer and diver, you played Division 1 tennis—none of these things are likely for the healthiest of men. You fought through incredible odds to achieve on the tennis courts and won matches you should have never won. You used your mind and will to defeat players who were definitely superior. You found a way. You always found a way.

We were married at an absurdly young age. We grew up together and overcame adversities on most every front. We were too young, we were financially strapped, we both had emotional baggage and psychological scars, we had years of schooling to get through. Well, we were also fiercely determined to take care of each other, to build a life together, to love each other and the beautiful children we were blessed to have in our lives. We were also blessed with incredible role models who taught us by example how to navigate this life. Always, we had examples, good and bad, of how to survive and how to thrive. We watched, we studied, and we learned. I pray we are still learning, because this life takes no prisoners and we are not through yet.

November 1, 2014, was a game-changer for us all. The elevator started down the shaft and it appeared that the brake was gone. The months that followed were a blur of hospital visits, decisions, forms, more decisions, more hospital visits, tears, fears, and confusion. Through it all, we prayed, we cried, we laughed, we talked, we raged against the darkness, and we prayed some more. We leaned on God; we leaned on our friends, our children, and each other. Just when we reached the breaking point, hope would knock on the door, faith would smash through a window, and despair would beat a hasty retreat just long enough for us to breathe. Grace would be more than sufficient; it would fill us up with a sense of wonder and peace that was inexplicable. We were surrounded by angels and we knew it. We were exactly where we were supposed to be and we accepted it. It was an adventure we were privileged to experience, no matter the outcome, no matter the cost, because no matter what happened, we had already won.

This life, your life, has unfolded according to divine design and plan. I am so blessed and so unendingly grateful to have been chosen to share this crazy roller-coaster existence with you. Against all odds, you are not just still standing, but are flourishing. I cannot wait to see what happens next, my darling Ed.

All my love, always and forever,
Paige

LISA MINK: TRANSPLANT NURSE
(BY ED)

In Colorado when you buy a pickup, a dog is included. When you qualify for the heart transplant list, a transplant nurse is assigned to you. He or she is with you the whole way, either way. I like to say that I was lucky enough to get a new heart, luckier still to be assigned to Lisa Mink.

I met Lisa on the day I was accepted into the transplant evaluation program. Less than two minutes after first laying eyes on her, serious quantities of blood were being drawn. Before the first vial with the tiny blue label was full, Lisa knew she had a problem. Ed was "one of those"! Heck, he can barely let us draw blood; what's he going to do when we do something actually serious?

Ninety-three days later, it was Lisa who called to say that a matching heart had been found. Ninety-three days. Seemed like an eternity to us; must have seemed like a life sentence to her. At first I used to say that I was her only patient, because she made me feel that way. As time went on, at rehab, clinic, and support group meetings, I met some of her other charges. When they spoke of her, I could see in their eyes a glimmer of hope peeking through overwhelming doubt. In their voices I could almost hear Lisa explaining why they felt this way or what the medicine would do or what was likely to happen next. Delivering pessimistic forecasts wins few followers; being overly hopeful is to bet against the house. We all read the same booklet. We knew that half of us would die before a good used heart arrived. We knew that one in eight would not survive the surgery even if a matching heart was found in time. We were painfully aware of the risk of stroke, infection, and acute rejection and that the luckiest of the lot would have a lifetime of spooky meds and uncertain life expectancies. Lisa found a way to make the pending minefield seem more like an achievement test.

After I got my new heart, a series of biopsies were to follow. I will not pretend I was brave and dignified. I was neither. The first four were weekly; the next eight were every other week, then monthly, and so on. A total of sixteen in the first year. These bothered me so much that within a day of finishing one, I began to fret and fear the next one. Lisa tried everything: IV sedative to take the edge off, but my veins were still bruised, burst, or already full of holes. OK, let's try an injection for the mild sedation just as they wheel me into the cath lab. A quick shot in the hip and the sedative wears off in forty-five minutes; what could go wrong? Despite Lisa's best efforts, within just a few minutes of my injection, both cath labs were taken over with serious emergencies that lasted several hours. By the time I was in the lab, the injection had long since worn off, and I was seriously dehydrated. Not a pleasant procedure, and Lisa felt worse than I did.

When I entered the evaluation program, I had barely six months to live. The medicine I began taking by infusion (through a semi-permanent port, administered via external pump that I carried 24/7) chemically forced my heart to beat stronger but reduced what time I had left by a third. I clearly remember being in clinic and Lisa explaining why my liver was enlarged, why I had a terrible taste in my mouth, why the back of my hands were turning black, why my skin was becoming covered with a rash, why I was losing bone and muscle, why my second pacemaker kept going off, why I couldn't leave town, why my left nipple was getting enlarged, why I kept getting weaker, why I had fluid in my lungs, and why my weight kept going down. I got honest answers from someone who believed in me.

Privacy rules prevent us patients from being told about others, even others struggling in the same way we struggle. But without a word being said, I could read the sorrow in Lisa's eyes when one of her patients was not going to make it. And when she found a good match for a worthy host, you could sense the joy in her eyes and in everyone else on the transplant floor.

Just a few weeks ago, I got to walk my daughter down the aisle at her wedding and take her hand and put it into the hand of a young man I really admire. Lisa Mink helped make that possible. Not sure just a thank-you note will do.

PART 4

Why Me, Lord?

*"Tell me, what is it you plan to do with
your one wild and precious life?"*

—MARY OLIVER, "THE SUMMER DAY"

No one is more surprised or delighted than I to be writing about Ed's life two years and twelve days after he received the gift of a new heart. As with everyone who inhabits this world, lots has happened. We have had incredible joy and unspeakable sorrow, overcome tremendous challenges, and delighted in beautiful experiences. In short, just like the rest of humanity, we have lived.

I listen to the Garth Brooks channel on Sirius in my car. Besides enjoying the artists featured along with Garth's songs, there are little anecdotes by Garth about music, his family, songwriting, and lessons learned along the way. He told about a sunrise horseback ride with two of his buddies one day in Oklahoma, just three guys enjoying the time together at a magical time of day. One of his buddies asked Garth if he knew the difference between mercy and grace. The friend then said (and I am paraphrasing here, but this is the gist of it) mercy is God not giving us what we deserve; grace is God giving us what we do not deserve.

When our youngest daughter, Laura Paige, was flying back to Denver three days after coming to Austin the day of Ed's transplant, she was walking through the terminal at Austin Bergstrom Airport, pushing her one-year-old daughter in a stroller. "The Live Music Capital of the World" frequently has live music going on in the concourse. As LP walked by a young musician singing in one of the bar areas, she spotted a familiar face. Kris Kristofferson was sitting alone at a tiny table, listening to the music. Laura Paige wheeled Eleanor right up to the table, introduced herself and her baby girl, and told Mr. Kristofferson how much she had enjoyed his music her entire life. He was gracious. He said he was terribly flattered that such a young, beautiful girl even knew who he was. They chatted and took a selfie together with Eleanor; she thanked him and left to catch her plane, thrilled to have met one of our family's music idols. Of course, what Kris Kristofferson did not know was that "Why Me, Lord?" pretty much describes Ed Innerarity's life. The words of that song capture the pathos, wonder, humility, and gratitude all of us experienced before, during, and after Ed became the steward of his new heart.

Ed has always stressed stewardship with our children. Being custodian of a new heart is an honor, a joy, and a huge responsibility. He has always lived a life filled with activity, projects, plans, and purpose. He is incredibly intense and focused. I guess the difference now is that his focus has changed a bit. Figuring out "Why Me, Lord?" has taken up lots of Ed's time. Some of that time he spends writing letters.

These letters are thank-you notes. These letters are lengthy. Ed writes to people from his past, going back all the way to his childhood. He thanks people who have made a difference in his life. He recounts specific ways he was molded and influenced by their friendship and efforts to mentor him. He writes letters to friends who have lost family members. He recounts memories of time with the men and women who shared their lives with him and expresses his appreciation and love for their lives as they intersected his. For a guy who claims that he cannot write his way out of a paper bag, he does a pretty good job. Of course, if you have made it to this point of the book, you know that to be true.

Ed goes to Seton Hospital and sees people who are waiting for a heart. He encourages them, he listens to them, and sometimes, if they have been friends for a while, he prays with them. No, he doesn't just bop around the hall of the cardiac ICU cold-calling strangers. These are visits with people he knows and loves.

Keeping up with the staff and medical professionals who have shepherded us to this point is a joy. When we go to Austin for Ed's check-ups, which are fewer all the time, it is a great reunion. The friendships we have made are deep and wide. We count on handshakes and hugs from Harvey when we park our car, welcoming smiles and more hugs and handshakes in the holding area before Ed goes back to the cath lab for his biopsy. Grace and mercy abound—undeserved but so appreciated by us. Ed usually gets by to see the physical therapists just to catch up with them while we are there, as well as Dr. Cishek's office to see everyone there. These men and women have all been integral players in a game that went down to the buzzer. We cannot ever tell them enough what they mean to us.

While Ed and the rest of our family have the bliss of more birthdays, more milestones, more living, other families are grieving. There was not enough medicine, not enough time, not a matching organ to save a life. Organ donation is profound and simple. Donating organs is donating life. Ed can never do enough to earn the gift of life. I can never do enough to show my gratitude for having my husband restored to me. All we can do is be kinder, be more generous, be better stewards of this time we never expected to receive, and urge others to donate Life. This was the reason we have shared these emails and this story.

From: Ed Innerarity
Sent: Monday, December 14, 2015 5:03 PM
Subject: "Home team bats last"

To All:

Imagine that Santa really did come to your house with a Dr. Seuss size sleigh full of all the things you ever wanted. A puppy, those shoes, a vacation, a grandchild, new snow skis, whatever. All of those things, especially the important ones. Paige and I got that and more Friday before last at the annual Seton Hospital Transplant Christmas Party. Again, imagine being in a room with dozens and dozens of people who openly shared their hopes and fears, their pain and joy, their despair and their gratitude, each in their own way and in their own words. No two stories were the same, but many reflected what it is to be looking over the cliff from which there is no chance of survival only to have your death sentence taken away. Each story was unique to that recipient and it was like hearing it for the first time as the microphone was passed from one ugly Christmas sweater to the next. Sometimes the joy and appreciation overwhelmed that person so much they could not finish. Often his or her spouse struggled for the words after being so close to losing their loved one.

In some ways, I was not a team player. I like people as much as the next guy, but on the diving board or tennis court, you are not shoulder-to-shoulder with others wearing the same color jersey. Last Friday was different. I am walking through the same minefield with every man and woman and every spouse in the McFadden Auditorium. (Not to mention all of those with a heart pump or heart mate. In many ways, their road is rockier still.) I told someone recently that the initiation was difficult but this is the coolest group I am a member of. Not all of us made it; I am told that I almost did not. But what we may have lacked in previous heart function has more than been made up with appreciation. Appreciation for our donor and his family, for the miracle of science that made this even a dream. Appreciation for those that supported us during our travails. Appreciation for today and then tomorrow. For each new day.

The last guy to speak was an eloquent black Baptist minister, although I think that is redundant. Some years ago, he received a new heart from a donor named Darrel. The reverend's words moved me to tears; then he introduced his guests, Darrel's sister and mother. You can only imagine.

I struggle to find the words to describe the Texas size pile of gifts heaped on our table last Friday. Each day, I have trouble finding the words just in conversations with myself. Think this is why I have shared those songs with you.

Live well and Merry Christmas to all of you.

ed

To those of you that ask about the music: there is no single song that perfectly matches the thoughts and emotions for all that I went through with the transplant. "Heart of Gold" came close. So did "Why Me, Lord." Just like there are no words to describe how we feel with our newborn child, or how we might feel in the middle of a stream late in the evening.

Admittedly, I have included today a song that you might have to think about to see how, or if, it fits this situation. It did for me. By coincidence, Buck Owens died in Bakersfield (and of heart problems no less). And that is Flaco Jiménez on the accordion. (The song is "Streets of Bakersfield.")

The other song is pretty obvious ("One Love"). RIP Bob and Buck. And Happy Birthday, Paige.

[*Songs #13 and #14.* Attached to this email were links to "Streets of Bakersfield" by Dwight Yoakum with Buck Owens and "One Love" by Bob Marley.]

ECMO: An extracorporeal membrane oxygenation (ECMO) machine provides both cardiac and respiratory support outside the body to persons whose heart and lungs cannot provide an adequate amount of gas exchange to sustain life. The ECMO drains blood from the vein, adds oxygen and removes carbon dioxide, warms the blood, returns the blood to the artery, and pumps the blood through the body. This machine allows the blood to bypass the heart and lungs.

From: Ed Innerarity

Sent: Wednesday, May 18, 2016 11:40 AM

Subject: "I did not come this far only to come this far"

Fellow runners,

I am a very fortunate guy.

My mother died of CHF a little over 10 years ago. Watching her struggle at the end just to breathe was one of the hardest things I ever had to do. Right after her service, I got checked out to see if I had "it" too. "It" is a genetic trait that causes cardiomyopathy, a gradual loss of the heart's ability to pump blood. It often leads to death from acute congestive heart failure, as it did in my mother's case. I am fortunate because I got checked out early and while the end point would be the same, its arrival might be deferred. I was also fortunate because when I was diagnosed, I was told that I would not die of old age. With certain meds and exercise, I could fully enjoy the 5, 10, or 15 years I had left. I decided right then, I would try to make the most of the finite but as yet undetermined number of life units I had left. I already had significantly reduced heart function, but I still did life. All the life I could. I did my elliptical training. I fished and hiked in Colorado. Babe and I hunted birds. I still walked when I played golf. I even climbed Half Dome a few years ago. I was very fortunate. The doctor said my body had compensated. My cardiomyopathy life was as full as most and probably more so.

I was fortunate because I began to pay more attention to life. I never took a single round of golf for granted. Whenever I broke 80, I wondered if it might be my last time to do so. I knew each trip to the mountains might be my last if I became unable to breathe, which I did. Later, I cut back on backpack trips in case I developed an irregular heart rhythm, which I did. I all but stopped taking fishing, golfing, or hunting trips out of town because of the ever more frequent episodes of acute dyspnea. Hard to enjoy a nice trip if you can't walk across the hotel lobby without having to sit and catch your breath. Hard to feel very manly if you can't open the door, pull back her chair, or carry the luggage for your wife. As I got closer to the end, I looked just like my dying mother, unable to breathe, but I did not lose my appreciation for each day. I did not come this far only to come this far.

I'm a very fortunate guy. As Graham Nash said, I have more than what I wanted. OK, I always wanted to dance and speak like Ricky Ricardo, but besides that.

And then some man died, and his family carried out his wishes. His heart was to be donated. And then some really fine doctors decided I was a perfect match, or perhaps his heart was a perfect match for me. And the next thing you know, his heart is in my chest. Right now, his heart is pumping blood through my body, allowing these thoughts to be written.

So here it is, coming up on 11 months. I plan on being so busy this summer, I will probably forget the actual anniversary date. I am so sure.

And I am sure America will elect a president this year that we all adore. I've been fortunate to be able to spend these past 11 months doing mostly what I want and what I need to do. Lots of rest for a while there. Lots of rehab although it is pretty much the same routine I did most of my adult life. Try to stay fit; you never know what might come up. Lots of reflection of how I got to where I am.

Since I was eight or nine years old, I liked the idea of a pecan orchard. Maybe it's too late, but over this past winter, I planted 50 new young pecan trees to go with the decades-old trees on our farm. This spring I took small branches from the best pecan varieties and grafted them onto some of my new young trees. Everything was going so well. Then a tornado hit our farm in March and did quite a job on some of our 100-plus-year-old trees. I took branches ripped off by the storm and spliced those onto young trees as well. Our very largest and oldest pecan tree, the one our logo is based on, took a direct hit by the twister. This stately 150-year-old gal lost two-thirds of her branches. We had to use the tractor to haul off thousands of pounds of limbs and I feared the worst for that tree. But she had not endured since the Civil War, provided shade for the Wichita, Comanche, and Caddo, witnessed the passing of the jaguar and the bison, and provided food for deer, turkeys, and feral hogs just to be finished off by an F1.

I wasn't necessarily very good at grafting, especially at first. Somehow, just being out there by myself, splicing parts of one tree onto another, was enough reward. Almost enough. And this past week at the farm, I noticed the first of the grafted scion wood had taken. And some day, that small native pecan tree will produce nuts genetically identical to the donor tree. I like that. It makes me realize how fortunate I am.

Live well, like part of you will be grafted onto somebody else someday.

ed

Today's song is "Long May You Run." This was written in the early '70s, after CSN had broken up, and was actually played at the Vancouver Winter Olympics in 2010.

[Song #15. Attached to this email was a link to "Long May You Run" by Neil Young.]

From: David Koch
Sent: Wednesday, May 18, 2016 12:34 PM
Subject: Re: "I did not come this far only to come this far"

Ed—thanks again for sharing your amazing insights . . . your words are inspiring and moving and I treasure what you have shared . . . I hope you know that you were never alone in your journey . . . let's go as fast as we can for as far as we can!!!

From: Lisa Mink
Date: Wednesday, May 18, 2016 9:39 PM
Subject: Re: "I did not come this far only to come this far"

To date, my favorite story you've written. Thanks for including me in your emails. I feel special!

Lisa

~~√~~√~~

From: Ed Innerarity
Sent: Friday, July 1, 2016 10:35 PM
Subject: One year ago

"In every walk with Nature,
one receives far more than he seeks."
—JOHN MUIR

Dear Friends and Family,

One year ago, almost to the hour, I was being prepared for my surgery. I was about to embark on the biggest challenge of my life as well as the greatest adventure. You guys pretty much know what has happened in the last year. My recovery has not been linear but almost everything in the past year has been good. The friends I met in the transplant program have been through difficulty but are inspirational examples for me to try to follow. I have really learned a lot from one such friend, who is really struggling. He is looking down the well of his own mortality. Though they were not part of my program, in the past few months, I have attended memorial services for a couple of transplant recipients that have gone on to Glory. I have learned much from their battles as well.

This is when I usually turn to John Denver or George Harrison to help me with the words that escape me. But not this time, I am on my own. I was pretty much finished writing these updates, but the one-year anniversary was too big to ignore. I made a point of going fly fishing late this evening, in the rain and overcast and mosquitoes, to be on the river, fly rod in hand at precisely the same time I sent you guys my Day Ninety-three update, just outside the operating room. For those of you that do not know me well, this is not about fish, maybe not even fishing. It is rather how I feel, with my favorite fly rod, alone on the river with My Creator, witnessing His majesty, His very fingerprints on every drop of rain, on every cloud that hangs on the mountains beside me, on every bit of white water on the river and part of every creature that calls this place home. I choose to physically be here tonight just as I was in spirit exactly one year ago. I am sure you all have your own such places; perhaps the beach, a farm or ranch, the lake, maybe an old church. Probably not the dentist.

All of you helped me get back here and I thank you from the bottom of my new heart.

I like to close by saying "live well, like . . ." I would like each of you to finish this one for me. I would love to hear how you would complete that sentence.

Living well,

ed

From: Lisa Mink
Sent: Saturday, July 2, 2016 12:50 AM
Subject: Re: One year ago

Ed,

Happy one year "heart-a-versary," Ed. And many, many more!

Say hi to the orcas for me. And for old times' sake, I will get the 20-gauge IV ready for the next time you're in clinic!

"Live well, like you've been given a second chance at life."

Much love,
Lisa

From: Caroline Cowden
Sent: Saturday, July 2, 2016 7:16 AM
Subject: Re: One year ago

Live well . . . like Ed!!!!! Your journey has been amazing and an incredible inspiration to me and so many others!!! I feel blessed to have been a small part of what you endured and the victorious outcome! Through it all, you never really thought about yourself. Your concerns were for your family, the donor, the donor's family, other people on the transplant list, and now, people who are facing what you were!!!! You appreciate every minute of every day and are eternally grateful to God for EVERYTHING! That is why I say live well like Ed!!!! Happy one year anniversary/birthday Ed!!!!

All my love,
Caroline

From: Winsome McIntosh
Sent: Saturday, July 2, 2016 9:17 AM
Subject: Re: One year ago

Dear Ed,

I knew you were a gifted fisherman. I knew you were a gifted oilman. I knew you were a gifted family man. I knew you were a gifted communicator. Until your health crisis, I didn't know what a gifted writer you are. We've exchanged these "updates" for events stretching from 2014 to now and I am so very grateful to be a part of your cheering squad.

Live Well with grace and courage to meet life's challenges and share/help others along the way . . . just like Ed.

See you soon in Alaska!

Winsome

From: Rebecca Innerarity
Sent: Saturday, July 2, 2016 3:28 PM
Subject: Re: One year ago

"Live well, like our Creator intended us to live."

Rebecca

From: David Hurta
Sent: Saturday, July 2, 2016 4:57 PM
Subject: Re: One year ago

Happy birthday, Ed. From now on, I won't think about how old you are; I will remember how new you are. Today, you are one year new!

Continue to live well, my good friend, and continue to live long.

David.

From: David Koch
Sent: Saturday, July 2, 2016 6:25 PM
Subject: Re: One year ago

Ed—thanks for your messages of inspiration . . . we should all live well . . .
and celebrate each day as the day we have been reborn . . . celebrate the
most amazing of all anniversaries!

david

From: David Terreson
Sent: Monday, July 4, 2016 5:54 PM
Subject: Re: One year ago

Ed,

I was thinking about your note the other day when our minister made
the comment in church "God is not through writing your story." Seems
clearly obvious in retrospect, less so on the front end or in the middle.
The impact you have had with sharing your story, your courage, and selflessness on everyone fortunate enough to have been around is unique
and a blessing to all of us.

I'd say "Live well—like it matters." Because it does—you are a testa-
ment to that.

David Terreson

From: Monica Gose
Sent: Tuesday, July 5, 2016 7:44 PM
Subject: Re: One year ago

Ed,

I say Live well—with your mind, body, and soul like there is no tomorrow. By looking at you I can see the possibilities are endless.

Love you,
Monica

From: Mickey Trimble
Sent: Thursday, July 7, 2016 3:20 PM
Subject: Re: One year ago

In response to your request to finish the sentence, I guess I would revise it a little and simply say, "Live well, today and every day to the Glory of our LORD."

MT

From: Ashley Wineinger
Sent: Monday, July 11, 2016 2:00 PM
Subject: Re: One year ago

Ed—

I would have to say "Live well, with depth."

Depth in relationships . . . saying what is on your heart and important, whenever you have the opportunity.

Depth of empathy . . . feeling strongly to others, in their great joys and in real sorrows and losses.

Depth in experiences . . . sucking the marrow out of life.

Depth of insight . . . really seeing; being a noticer.

Love,
Ashley

From: Jim Kemper
Sent: Sunday, July 10, 2016 4:37 PM
Subject: Favorite Verse, Favorite Movie

Ed—

The following thoughts came to me during our talks in the car, traveling between hunting spots in South Dakota. There's nothing like near-death life experiences and hunting together to conjure up meaningful, valuable conversation. It's taken this long for me to sit down and assemble it in writing. This anniversary seems as appropriate a time as any to share with you.

I have a tradition I've shared with each of my four children, whenever they turned 13 years old. The two of us go on a "grown up" ski trip, during which we take 4–5 days to study the book of Proverbs and discuss how to recognize the wise man, the fool, the scoffer, the seducer, etc. You taught me, when I was a teenager, how hunting and getting away on adventures allows time to figure out life. Every night, during my trips with my children, we would read and study the words that the wisest man in the world wrote to his child, to prepare that child for adulthood. After four trips, with four children, I've assembled several key verses, but from the beginning of the tradition, the verse that remains the theme verse and the "take-away" message is Proverbs 4:23.

The NIV [New International Version Bible] reads, *"Above all else,* guard your heart; for everything you do flows from it." There are many great translations . . . "Above all else, guard your heart; for it is the wellspring of life." King James reads, "Keep thy heart with all diligence; for out of it *are* the issues of life." I love this verse, especially for a 13 year old, because in one verse, it covers 31 chapters of Solomon's instructions to avoid the snares of life. Even now, when our family discusses struggles or someone is embarking on a journey or adventure, we can utter to one another just the first three words—"Above all else . . ." It is an understood warning, instruction, and expression of love, regarding what really matters more than anything. The Hebrew word for heart in this verse is the same one used in describing David as "a man after God's own heart." It's not talking about our heart of flesh, though the metaphor is not lost. David's soul, his priorities, his cares were patterned after God's. Ed, you are a Proverbs 4:23 man. A Proverbs 4:23 man cares more about the person he's chatting with than getting down the road to his next appointment. A Proverbs 4:23 man cares more about the legacy he leaves than making an extra buck or impressing somebody. He cares more about his purity and his heart than about feeling good or achieving some status or conquest. I got a ringside seat while a Proverbs 4:23 man underwent a heart transplant. Now, if that's not irony, I don't know what is. The last year reading your messages and revelations about life has so juxtaposed the drama of your heart's journey against the beauty of your soul's journey. I am not alone in saying, "thank you" for the way you've touched so many of us.

My favorite movie is *It's a Wonderful Life.* It always has been, despite all the advances in movie-making and special effects; I've never felt any story even comes close to that of George Bailey's epiphany and under-standing of life. It's a story and script so thick with metaphors and ironies. One of the reasons I love this movie is because George Bailey is every-one. I cannot relate to William Wallace, although I'd like to tell people I can. I'm not as smart as Tony Stark. I'm not as tough as Rocky Balboa. Sure, there are lots of movies where "ordinary men" become heroes or complete extraordinary feats. But William Wallace and Rocky are not, in my opinion, "ordinary guys." George Bailey *is really* an ordinary guy who really doesn't do any extraordinary things. George has wants similar to those the rest of us have ... *"Ah, I wish I had a million dollars ... Hot dog!"* (read with Jimmy Stewart flair). He wants to travel the world and see things and escape that crummy little town where he grew up. Like me, he periodically stumbles over the idea that there's something out there that's going to sate his desire for fun, adventure, and conquest.

George is a hard worker and a man with a plan. But, every time he gets things all lined up to embark on his adventure, his heart gets in the way. Whether it's tying the knot with the love of his life, helping out his neighbor, or bailing out the old Bailey Building & Loan, *above all else*, George listens to and follows the heart that God gave him. George is a Proverbs 4:23 guy. Like many of us, even if we were to set our priori-ties like George does, we may still miss the point. George had to die (or never be born) before Clarence Oddbody could lead him to appreciate the dividends produced by being a 4:23 man.

As I've talked with you, Ed, and read your wonderful thoughts on life and God, I can't help but think that you and George could really relate to each other:

"Strange isn't it? Each man's life touches so many other lives. When he isn't around, he leaves an awful hole, doesn't he?"

CLARENCE ODDBODY

I wouldn't claim to want to walk the journey you've walked over the past few years. It wasn't mine anyway. But, in some ways, I envy the clarity you've found. For some reason, God chose for you to face this journey, and you have walked it well. Maybe it is so you could see how many lives you've touched. Maybe so you could see how well you've lived Proverbs 4:23. You have been a great brother and, at times, a father for me. I celebrate this year milestone with you and I am thankful that you were born with the heart you've always had and still have.

—To my big brother, the richest man in town!

JK

LVAD: The left ventricular assist device (LVAD or VAD) is a kind of mechanical heart pump. It is placed inside a person's chest, where it helps the heart pump oxygen-rich blood throughout the body.

From: Ed Innerarity
Sent: Monday, May 29, 2017 9:52 PM
Subject: Wedding rings, labs, tuxedos: 3/1/17

Friends,

Like many of you, especially those of you in business, I am a rate-of-return guy. Meaning, I hope to get some positive return on my investment. Simple enough, even biblical. Dave Ramsey would certainly approve. Examples abound: hoping to get many years of dependable service from that washer/dryer set, a car that lasts longer than the car note, a fly rod that will last for years, a good dividend paying stock, the remodeled kitchen. You get the point. You could come up with as many good examples as I.

Not every investment we make and not every purchase of a durable good is expected to yield measureable returns. Like a tuxedo or a wedding ring. More about this later.

During the year or two leading up to my big new heart adventure, my life was the pits. My golf game too, although that seems so obvious as to barely require typing the words. Some of you knew of my problems, many were sympathetic, but not my golf buddies. They took great delight in winning $6 each Saturday as I was unable to will myself to be stronger. With each passing week, I was slipping further behind and further away. Behind the others and away from my former self and former life. Perhaps the worst part was that I had not yet accepted the fact that as my heart slowly headed south, it took with it my 7 iron. Then my putter, and then my driver. I could have just as easily said it took my joy. Then my dignity, and finally my hope. It's all the same.

I know holding my own on the golf course with these guys is not what I was put on the earth for, but in desperate times, you seek a familiar cave to wait out the storm.

So I get the call and a young grieving widow offers to let me borrow her husband's heart. That was exactly 600 days ago. Exactly one day ago, I got my 18th and final biopsy. It and almost all of the 17 before have gone well. Each one easier than the one before if that is possible. But unless I get sick or slip into a rejection episode, 18 of those trips to Disney World will be it.

And now for the part about me. During the past 600 days, I have had a chance to see up close what a second chance at life looks like. And

I have shared some of what that's like already. Not all of that has been smooth sailing, but I am no longer in a leaking lifeboat. During this time I got shingles like many others get, and I had to have a rather nasty and scary skin cancer cut out. Many transplant recipients experience that. And yesterday I had an MRI along with my Two for Tuesday biopsy which confirmed a ruptured disc squished between L-5 and L-4. Like we really care what the L it is next to. This hurt more than the transplant or my knee replacement, and I don't even know how I did it. It hurt so bad I found myself calling out to Jesus for help. Since that call did not go through, I found myself wondering if there is something to be learned from all this pain. It sure would be a waste of everyone's time to have a pain that bad without something important to be learned. I told a friend that I finally figured out the lesson only to be told that I had called them only a few days earlier with a different lesson. OK then, pain so bad, it comes with two lessons. My original theory was that I was being shown what Paige might be going through since her wreck several years ago. But that wouldn't make sense because this is supposed to be about me.

The lesson I am to learn is how I lived the past 600 days. OK, most of the time, I was sufficiently grateful and thankful and appreciative, but I also found ample time to do rehab on my pride. During these 600 days, I was very diligent about doing everything they told me to do regarding post-transplant rehab. "Slow and steady and make it part of your daily/weekly routine until it is a habit." I have done strength training 132 times since my transplant. I record each one on a chart inside a blue folder with my name on it in a big clear plastic organizer behind the folder with Paige's name. 132 trips in all kinds of weather, and I recorded each machine I used that day and how many reps and how many sets, and when I finally got to slightly increase the weight under the watchful eye of the main PT guy. Plus treadmill sessions. Of course, I was just doing what I was told. OK, I was doing a few more of them than maybe I was told to do. But this was my ticket back to where I had been 10 years ago. I could play with our granddaughter, I could hunt with David and Jim and Jamison and Brian, I could hike with everybody up in Colorado, I could get back in the river that is my soul, and I could play golf again, perhaps like before. I kept telling myself the more I put in, the more I will get out. More of that return on investment thing.

Pride did not turn my rehab into something bad; pride stole why I was doing it at all. Nothing wrong at all about getting back into shape, nothing wrong at all. I just seemed to forget that while my heart is 30-something years old, my knees, hips, and discs are 65. I also seemed to forget that 132 workouts or a thousand, none of them were possible without the donor family, the folks at Seton, my supportive family and friends, and a million things that could have gone wrong, but haven't. Not yet anyway.

One drawback to living 300 miles from the transplant hospital is that it is harder to stay in touch with the others in the program. Nurses and doctors, techs, and IV "cultists" I get to see most every visit. But the others who experienced the same or similar struggles as I, those guys I miss. And the ones whose struggles and ordeals were far worse, my heart really goes out to them.

OK, back to the tux and wedding ring. On those investments, there is a different kind of return, one that is realized even without having to sell it. But who sells a used tuxedo or wedding ring? Many of these thoughts came to me as we were planning to attend the wedding of our sweet niece. I even ordered a new tux, pretty sure that I would not have a chance to wear it enough times to offset the cost of renting one. Some investments have returns far greater than percentages can measure. Tuxedos. Wedding rings. Letting someone have your organs when you are through.

Ed's Note: This was written on February 28th but not sent to you guys because of the disc issues. I found out the next day that I would not be able to attend the special wedding because I got the unhappy disc surgically repaired. I also lost another one of my fellow transplant guys after a very long and very arduous battle. It is a very humbling experience to be part of a group of men and women desperately trying to stay alive long enough for a transplant, or an LVAD, only to witness their battle with endless complications. Particularly when my transplant went so smoothly. Like I said, pretty humbling.

Live well, like your joints are young again.

ed

THE THIRD DAVID
(BY PAIGE)

One of the greatest blessings of Ed's illness has been David Terreson. When Ed was diagnosed with cardiomyopathy, we had all of the test results sent to my brother, Jim Kemper, who is an otologist in Austin. Jim, who is our in-family consultant on all medical questions, read everything carefully. Ed's woefully low ejection fraction was only one of many red flags but was particularly alarming. In his kind, measured way, Jim told Ed he wanted him to "come as soon as possible to Austin and see my friend David Terreson. He is a fantastic cardiologist and a great guy. I want him to check you out. This needs to be done now, Ed."

Truer words have never been spoken. David Terreson and his wife, Pam, have shared their lives with us now for over ten years. There was an immediate rapport between David and Ed that was brought about by shared interests in hunting, fly fishing, economics, sports, and the fact that their wives became fast friends, hiking all over the mountains while the boys pursued trout on float trips and wet wading. David has a disarming self-deprecating manner and humor, is a terrific chef, and possesses an encyclopedic knowledge of the human heart. His medical training is superior, and his Pascagoula, Mississippi, accent belies a razor-sharp intellect. He and Pam have been steadfast friends, gracious hosts, incomparable guests, and delightful adventurers with us for many summers in Austin, Midland, and Colorado.

The fact that David Terreson was able to keep Ed's flaccid, worn-out heart beating for almost ten years after taking over his case is a credit to his skill as a doctor and Ed's compliance as a patient. The only time they really had a disagreement was over Ed's determination to climb Half Dome.

Ed has read every word written by the great naturalist John Muir. His book *My First Summer in the Sierra* lit a fire within my husband of evangelical intensity. Ed started training to climb Half Dome, the signature granite monolith of Yosemite National Park.

Climbing Half Dome is done by people of varying fitness levels and completed by many of them successfully. The last five hundred feet of the climb, up metal cables for one's hands and boards at forty-foot intervals for one's feet, is extremely rigorous. Of course, that is after hiking eight miles to the base of Half Dome. Once the summit is attained and pictures are taken, "what goes up must come down," and the climber has to descend along the same cables. All of this ascending and descending is accompanied by scores of other climbers of varying abilities, putting one another in varying degrees of peril. Dry granite is slippery. Wet granite is deadly slick. People die on Half Dome every year due to ill-preparation, poor conditioning, lightning strikes, inclement weather, their own carelessness or that of other climbers, or just bad luck. Ed could not wait to get to Yosemite!

Of course, he shared this awesome plan with his outdoorsy friend and doctor, David. David told him there was no way that any of those people who had climbed Half Dome had advanced cardiomyopathy. Ed would be putting his life at tremendous risk. He would be in a wilderness area where he could not be evacuated in a timely manner. The elevation change in a single day is 4,800 feet. Ed needed to realize this was a dangerous idea and forget about it.

God bless David Terreson. He called me. He urged me to try to reason with Ed. I told David that I understood his concerns. I knew they were valid. I told him that there was no way I could discourage Ed from attempting the climb.

Life is fleeting and precious. Our experiences validate and confirm our appreciation of each breath we take. We are all living on borrowed time. The difference with Ed was he knew his time was very limited. Heart disease would kill him, more likely sooner than later. He was racing mortality to squeeze every last glorious moment in before it was too late. "Die Trying" was the name of his drift boat and his motto. I would not kill his spirit by trying to deny him the chance to climb that iconic American symbol of the wilderness he loved.

Ed climbed Half Dome. A framed picture of Ed, standing on top of Half Dome with his arms outstretched in triumph, sits in a place of honor on David's desk.

From: Paige Innerarity
Sent: Sunday, January 29, 2017
Subject: Daniel

Dear Lisa,

Ed told me that when he spoke with you today he learned that Daniel had died. Daniel, who I met one time because we were at the same table at the Christmas luncheon at Seton. Daniel, who was wheeled down from his hospital room connected to a whole cartload of IVs, monitors, and medical devices, just like Ed had been when he was being evaluated as a transplant candidate. But not at all like Ed, because Daniel's lips were blue; he was incredibly weak, wrapped in multiple blankets and layers to keep him warm; and he could barely whisper "hello" when we all introduced ourselves. Ed was never that thin, that sick, that hollow-eyed. Daniel, whose sweet wife filled a plate with food from the buffet, encouraging him to eat, watching his every move, his every breath, with love. I remember doing that. I remember trying to be available but not hovering, helpful but not smothering, walking a tightrope over a minefield of my own and Ed's emotions. I don't think I did it with the grace of Daniel's wife. No, I am sure I didn't.

I was deeply impressed with both of them. I thought Daniel and his wife incredibly brave to come to the luncheon when he was so sick. They didn't know any of us in that room, except you and some of the other hospital folks who were all working like crazy to try and save his life. We tried, not too successfully, to engage them in conversation. Perhaps we didn't try hard enough. Perhaps they just wanted to sit there, be part of a Christmas lunch, and feel included. Dear God, I hope they felt included. I do remember being amazed when Daniel whispered that his father had received a heart transplant. I hope his father had a good outcome. Daniel did not say, and we did not ask.

When we passed the microphone around the room, and it was Daniel's turn, he waved it away and covered his face with his hands. I wanted to climb under the table. His wife took the microphone from him and said, "This is my husband, Daniel. We have noticed that everyone who has received a transplant has a number. We hope that Daniel will be getting a number very soon." Anyone and everyone who heard that statement must have held that same hope, looking at that dear couple who shared so honestly their vulnerability, fear, and deepest desire with us.

Ed was the 382nd transplant at Seton, and the 13th transplant for 2015. Only because some individual, or a grieving family, stepped up and made the offer of life did Ed get his number, his chance to live. Daniel never received his number and I cannot stop thinking about him.

Lisa, I cannot thank you enough for the job you do. I cannot thank any of you at the transplant center adequately, and it is ludicrous for me to try, but I will never stop trying. My job, Ed's job, our family's job is to beat the drums, ring the bells, and tell the world to DONATE LIFE. It is not enough to be grateful, ever. Daniel did not get his number, and that is reason enough to tell the world there are too many people who die waiting for that phone call from the transplant center.

If you happen to see Daniel's wife, tell her that we are grieving for her today. Tell her that she and Daniel made a deep and lasting impression on Ed, Sarah, Cameron, and me. Tell her, she is in our prayers tonight and for many nights to come. Whether she even remembers meeting us is so incredibly unimportant. What is important is that we remember her, and we will always remember Daniel.

Ejection fraction: A measurement of the percentage of blood leaving the heart with each contraction.

EPILOGUE

Both Sides, Now

Paige, July 23, 2017

Written by Joni Mitchell in 1967, "Both Sides, Now" has been recorded by many artists of virtually every genre. Judy Collins recorded it after hearing the young songwriter sing it to her over the phone from an agent's office the year it was written. It was a hit. Subsequently, Joni recorded it herself in 1969. Bing Crosby and Carly Rae Jepsen recorded it, as did Willie Nelson. The song has always been dear to me. It has layers and depth that show incredible insight, particularly when considering that Joni Mitchell was only twenty-four years old when she penned it. As she sings of clouds, then love, then life in the three verses, the listener is pulled into the writer's philosophical musings and arrives at the same conclusion: We really don't know clouds, love, or life at all.

The events of our lives shape each of us. Choices are made; people influence us for better or worse, depending on our perceptions, our backgrounds, our desire to learn from experience. I believe in the power of love over hate, of good over evil. I also believe that our time on earth is only part of our existence, that we only see through myopic lenses, rarely seeking the long view. I do not pretend to know why Ed was one of the fortunate ones. I thank God he lived, and I grieve for everyone who died waiting to receive a heart or whatever lifesaving organ that did not become available in time.

As for the donor families, how can we ever live well enough and be grateful enough? We cannot. We just cannot do it. For Ed and our family, sympathy became empathy in October 2016. We see from Both Sides, Now.

Once upon a time, there lived a family. The father, Patrick, and the mother, Erin, loved each other very much. They had two beautiful children: Hicks and Mary Caroline. Hicks was a typical three-year-old boy. He was wild, carefree, funny, and mischievous. Hicks had the golden curls of a cherub and a twinkle in his eye that contradicted all angelic tendencies with one exception: his fierce yet tender love for his baby sister, Mary Caroline. "Sister" was his heart. From the time she arrived home from the hospital, Hicks was her protector, her entertainer, her devoted big brother. There was not a modicum of jealousy toward this blue-eyed angel who had displaced his rule as the "one and only." He didn't just accept her, he doted on her.

Patrick and Erin were wonderful parents. They spent time playing with their precious children, reading to them, teaching them. Patrick sang to Mary Caroline every night during her bath time. Her favorite song was "Sweet Baby James" by James Taylor. Erin was a wonderful wife and mother. She was sweet and energetic, laughing easily and forgiving quickly. This beautiful family was surrounded by a very large extended family of parents, brothers, sisters, aunts, uncles, cousins, and devoted friends. Everyone loved them because of their generous hearts, sense of fun, and sweet spirits.

Mary Caroline was a product and reflection of her family. She was incredibly secure and outgoing. Even though she was less than a year old, she expressed delight in everything the world had to offer. She laughed and waved excitedly at everyone, friends and strangers alike. As soon as she could stand and walk, she would dance to every tune she heard. With a smile on her face, she watched her brother and her cousins running and playing, as if she knew that before too long, she would be able to keep up with them. Mary Caroline was filled with joy.

One day, Mary Caroline became very sick. Realizing that something was terribly wrong, her parents took her to the hospital. Tests were run, and doctors and nurses worked around the clock to slow the bacterial infection, to make her well. After a couple of days, the unthinkable had become reality. In spite of her parents doing everything right, of doctors and nurses using all the best medical procedures known, Mary Caroline would never resume life in this world. On October 12, 2016, Mary Caroline joined other saints and angels in paradise.

Erin and Patrick's family and friends gathered around them. They came to show their love, their support, and to be together to share their sorrow. Because this was a very large, loving, and strongly connected family, something very unusual happened. Though tears were shed, there were times of laughter. The joy that was the hallmark of Mary Caroline's short life filled the waiting room. The hospital staff said they had never seen anything like it. Many of them joined the family during their time off duty to listen to the conversation. The family members thanked them, every doctor and nurse they encountered, for their heroic efforts to save Mary Caroline. It was a strange and spiritual time.

When Patrick's aunt arrived, he met her with a big hug. After thanking her for coming, the first words he said were "Paige, Erin and I have donated Mary Caroline's organs." Paige and Patrick hugged again, for a very long time. After that, they walked back to Mary Caroline's room so Paige could hold her tiny, perfect hand and tell her good-bye. Of course, Mary Caroline's beautiful soul had already left her body and flown straight to heaven, but Paige knew that heaven is closer than we think and that this Joy Child could hear every word.

For several days, the family and friends gathered at the hospital. Back in Mary Caroline's room, Erin, Patrick, Chris (Erin's brother), Kemper and Craig (Patrick's brothers), and Mary Caroline (Patrick's sister) took turns staying with their precious angel. Hicks spent time with his devoted and beloved grandmothers (Peggy and Caroline), aunts, uncles, and sweet cousins in a never-ending cycle of confusion, distraction, and love. The last afternoon in the hospital, Patrick and Erin were alone in their child's room to spend as much time with her as possible. As Patrick looked out the window, he told Erin, "From now on, I want to take the time to really appreciate every single moment. I want to experience life the way Mary Caroline did. I want to stop and watch the sunset with Hicks. I want to tell him how blessed we are to have a God who lóves us enough to create so much beauty for us to enjoy in this world. If we see a butterfly, I want to stop and really *see* that butterfly and be thankful for it." With that, a butterfly flew across the window in front of them.

For a minute, neither Erin nor Patrick spoke. Finally, Patrick said, "So, did you see something just now? If so, what did you see?"

Erin said, "I saw a butterfly, Patrick, just like you did."

Two days later, Highland Park United Methodist Church was filled with people from all over the country who gathered to celebrate the short but profoundly meaningful life of Mary Caroline Cowden. As the minister said, "She never had a bad day. Every day was filled with joy."

The following day, October 16, would have been Mary Caroline's first birthday. The Cowdens hosted a huge party at their house. Pink bows on every tree, pink balloons in every chair, a bouncy castle ("Because Sister would want a bouncy castle," according to Hicks), food, music, and lots of little girls wearing butterfly wings dominated the yard. The launching of dozens of pink balloons by people of all ages was glorious.

Months have passed, and life continues for this family. There remains a Mary Caroline-shaped hole in their lives that will always be there. In spite of water wells in Africa that have been dug in her memory, in spite of countless volunteer hours served in her memory, money poured into charities, and prayers for healing their broken hearts, they miss her. Faith, hope, and love will ultimately win, but they will always miss her, always remember her.

On the twelfth day of every month, many people remember Mary Caroline Cowden. In her memory, they find a way to share joy. It may be a phone call or visit to brighten someone's day, cookies delivered to a neighbor, groceries bought anonymously for a family in need, picking up the lunch tab of a complete stranger. People use their imaginations and do remarkably joyful deeds.

And somewhere, an unknown family is experiencing the joy of having their child restored to health. Mary Caroline's gift saved a life.

Life is a mystery. Life is filled with so many challenges, so much drama, so much adventure. Live well, live joyfully, and donate life.

ED'S EMAIL PLAYLIST

"Slip Slidin' Away" by Paul Simon, attached to emails dated April 9 and July 1, 2015

"Why Me, Lord?" by Kris Kristofferson, July 8, 2015

"Heart of Gold" by Neil Young, July 9, 2015

"The Air That I Breathe" by The Hollies, July 11, 2015

"Here Comes the Sun" by The Beatles, July 21, 2015

"Teach Your Children" by Crosby, Stills & Nash, July 23, 2015

"Take Me Home, Country Roads" by John Denver, July 31, 2015

"Blue Moon" by The Marcels, July 31, 2015

"The Road to Ensenada" by Lyle Lovett, August 2, 2015

"How Can You Mend a Broken Heart" by the Bee Gees, August 20, 2015

"Wasted on the Way" by Crosby, Stills & Nash, November 8, 2015

"Streets of Bakersfield" by Dwight Yoakum, December 14, 2015

"One Love" by Bob Marley, December 14, 2015

"Long May You Run" by Neil Young, May 18, 2016

BENEDICTION

"You go nowhere by accident. Wherever you go, God is sending you. Wherever you are, God has put you there; He has a purpose in your being there. Christ who indwells you has something He wants to do through you where you are. Believe this and go in His grace and love and power."

Richard C. Halverson
1916–1995
Presbyterian Minister
Former U.S. Senate Chaplain

ABOUT THE AUTHORS

Ed Innerarity is an observer of life. He is fascinated by science and frustrated with words. In eighth grade he mutated and cultured a strain of *E. coli* resistant to antibiotics for his science project.

After spending a large part of her childhood with her nose in a book, no one could be more surprised than Paige Innerarity to realize she has managed to help write one! When she is not reading and writing, Paige can be found designing jewelry; binge-watching various BBC series about murder, history, and baking; and hiking the trails above Creede, Colorado, with family, friends, and dogs.

Made in the USA
Lexington, KY
15 June 2018